Creation House is a ministry of Christian Life Missions. Its purpose is to publish and distribute Bibles, books and other Christian literature presenting the Gospel of Jesus Christ. If you would like additional information, we encourage you to write to us at 396 E. St. Charles Rd., Wheaton, IL 60188.

They
Marched to
HEAVEN'S
DRUMBEAT

They
Marched to
HEAVEN'S
DRUMBEAT

Clarence Finsaas

Creation House, Carol Stream, Illinois

Acknowledgements

This has been, to a great extent, a family project. My wife, Jeanette, has patiently listened as I have read and reread every chapter to her. Our daughter Renee Komlofske has done the typing. Our daughter Barbara Brody has been the proofreader. I owe much to my sister Lila Joseph, my aunt Alma Aarhus and a family friend, Marie Girard, for their suggestions and input. To each I express my sincere gratitude.

Excerpts from the following are used by permission:

Wingspread, by A.W. Tozer, Christian Publications.

The General Next to God, by Richard Collier, Dutton Publishing Co.

Bush Aglow, by Richard Ellsworth Day, Baker Book House.

Smith Wigglesworth: Apostle of Faith, by Stanley Howard Frodsham, Gospel Publishing House.

Oswald Chambers, His Life and Work, by Oswald Chambers, Simkin Marshall, Ltd.

Praying Hyde, by Frances A. McGaw, Bethany Fellowship, Inc.

An Irish Saint, by Helen E. Bingham, Evangelical Publishers, Inc.

All Bible quotations from the King James Version unless otherwise noted.

Published by Creation House, 396 E. St. Charles Rd.,
Carol Stream, IL 60188

In Canada: G.R. Welch, Ltd., 960 Gateway, Burlington,
Ontario, Canada L7L 5K7

Printed in the United States of America

ISBN 0-88419-193-1
Library of Congress Catalog Card Number (applied for)

CONTENTS

Foreward

This is a book about "spiritual renewal."
It is a book about "deeper life."
It is a book about "second blessing."
It is a book about "victorious Christian living."
It is a book about "being filled with the Holy Spirit."

All of this in one book, you ask? Yes, and more. Or, to look at it from another perspective, less!

Confusing? Not really. The subject of this book has been a source of misunderstanding and confusion, but when you read through it I believe that you will make the same delightful discovery that I did: behind man-made confusion the author shows us a pattern of truth that is divine simplicity itself.

The confusion comes when we take terms like "deeper life," or "being filled with the Holy Spirit" and try to make abstract doctrines out of them. In their origin, they were descriptions of personal experience.

Clarence Finsaas goes back to the source. He introduces us to 20 Christians, men and women, each of whom had a transforming spiritual experience. His sense of anecdote and his eye for detail bring the characters up off the page. He lets us see them, hear them, share in their struggles, and be encouraged by their faith.

We read the story of a Methodist circuit rider on the American frontier, or the story of a Catholic mystic, or the story of a Pentecostal evangelist. . .and inescapably we find ourselves saying: *"These people are all talking about the same thing!"*

Their religious backgrounds are different. They don't use the same religious vocabulary. But what *happens* to them— the reality itself, for all the uniqueness of each individual story—is arrestingly familiar. The further one reads, the more strongly the message comes through: these people are describing the same kind of thing—an intensified experience of the sovereign, living Christian experience that deepens devotion toward God and releases powerful ministry toward others.

What language *is* adequate to describe an encounter with the living God? These people described their experiences the best way that they could, given the tools of language, culture, and education that were available to them. The descriptions are different, but the reality is essentially the same.

Nothing confusing about that, unless we forget the reality and fall to quibbling about the way people describe it.

Clarence Finsaas helps move us beyond that kind of foolishness to a place where we can rejoice in the varied ways that men and women have experienced more deeply the reality of God, yes, and can say both in longing and in faith, "Lord, I need it too!"

Larry Christenson, Director
International Lutheran Renewal Center

Preface

The victorious Christian life. Is it reserved for only a gifted few? The 20 men and women highlighted in this book came from a wide variety of backgrounds. Yet all sought and obtained a "crowning experience" that more adequately fitted them for Christian life and service. They did not always use the same terminology, but they did speak a common language of the heart. What they called this experience depended on their individual backgrounds. They expressed themselves with the tools of speech nearest at hand. It could hardly be otherwise, for no one would try to explain his experience in words and terminology with which he was not familiar. A Presbyterian would not be apt to use the language of a Quaker in giving testimony to his deeper encounter with God. Nor would a Quaker's language necessarily be the same as that of Baptist.

Representative characters purposely have been taken from the whole spectrum of the Christian Church, Catholic to Pentecostal. There is a common denominator that unites them, and when this is understood the differences in the family of God will be minimized and overshadowed by the realization of a common bond.

We are impressed with how much these men and women had in common to begin with. This is as it should be. Spiritual pilgrimages are not that much different. Take the men of Bible times. Whether it was Joseph, Moses, or David, each had to be trained by God and tested under pressure before being entrusted with his pre-destined role in God's kingdom.

It wasn't enough to have a divine call. There were years of training. These were years of exposure, subtraction, and reorientation. They had to learn the total inadequacy of personal effort in doing battle against spiritual forces. When their trust was no longer in themselves but in God, they were ready to serve.

The process was the same for these believers of an earlier day. They were called, ushered into training, and then tested. In the process they began to see their self-centeredness and the uselessness of self effort. Struggles ensued. There was the inner dissatisfaction and outward discouragement. When the distress and darkness was at its zenith and hope all gone, the answer came. They saw God's provision. It was a word from the Scriptures, a letter from a friend, a phrase from a book or a song, but it was the key that unlocked the windows of heaven and faith broke forth in realization. So very simple.

Christ already had made them free. It was because they had failed to discover their freedom that they were kept in bondage.

Rev. Clarence B. Finsaas

1

A.B. Simpson (1843-1919)

Christian & Missionary Alliance

"**R**eligious Calisthenics" was what the biographer called it. It consisted of "church, family prayer, the catechism. . .long dry books by the reforming fathers, more prayer and church again."[1] That would seem like an incredible and well-nigh impossible Sunday schedule for the youth of today. The father would read from *Baxter, The Saints' Rest*, or from some other writer, and the children would listen. . .and they'd better not laugh. . .not on the Sabbath. The penalty was a whipping. In his latter years the grown man still remembered. . .with a trace of chagrin on his face. . .for in all their sincerity and religious austerity, no one had thought to steer the youth into God's corral. With the heavy burden of religious exercises, the hungry heart had not been tended to. He was yet unsaved.

Albert Simpson was born in Bayview, Prince Edward Island, Canada, on December 15, 1843. He was one of four children of James and Jane Simpson. Another son had died earlier and the mother, like Hannah of the Old Testament, had asked the

Lord for this boy. Should God grant her wish, she would lend him to the Lord, "that the boy might be a minister or a missionary if he lives and grows up and is so inclined."[2]

Jane Simpson is described as a "great soul, sensitive, poetic, beauty-loving, and with a soaring imagination." The fulfillment of her longings and dreams were throttled by the drab existence of Canadian farm life. She often would cry to herself, for she had known better days. She had been no stranger to culture, refinement, and the best of society. Reading the works of Milton, Scott, Cowper, Thompson and others brightened many otherwise dull days.

James was of more practical bent. A merchant, miller, and shipbuilder, he is described as "clean, capable, and industrious." He was a respected Presbyterian who had served as an elder of the church for more than half of his lifetime.

The Puritan austerity that seems to have been an important part of the Simpson household did not deter young Albert from answering the call to the ministry. His father had planned otherwise, but when the young lad spoke up in one of the family council meetings it became apparent to both father and mother that the hand of God was upon the boy. James was wise enough not to interfere. After all, the prophet Jeremiah was called to the ministry before *he* was born.

Young Simpson had a brilliant mind. Under a private tutor he began to study Latin, Greek, and higher mathematics. Later he enrolled in the Chatham High School, about nine miles from the Simpson home. He rode horseback to school, but many times, when no horse could be spared, he walked.

The physical and mental exertion, coupled with a lack of peace in his own heart, took a toll on the young boy, and he became very ill. Although in later years his physical health slowly returned, his mental state was one of distress. However, God was preparing His servant, and the dawn was near at hand.

It was while browsing among some books that he found a volume called *Marshall's Gospel Mystery of Sanctification*.

He had not been reading long when a paragraph leaped at him from the page. "The first good works you will ever perform," said the author, "is to believe on the Lord Jesus Christ. Until you do it, all your works, prayers, tears, and good resolutions are vain. To believe on the Lord Jesus Christ is to believe that He saves you according to His Word, that He receives and saves you here and now, for He has said, 'Him that cometh to me I will in no wise cast out.'"

In that moment young Simpson found peace. The shackles that had bound him vanished. He knelt down and, with an overflowing heart, accepted God's gift of salvation so generously offered to all men.

Having completed his high school courses, Simpson set his sights on a higher goal. Knox College would give him the academic and spiritual training needed to fit him for the ministry. But would Knox College have him?

The ruling body of Presbyterian elders didn't take just anyone. All applicants were screened. Why did the young candidates want to be ministers? Their answers had to be good.

It was a somewhat fearful day when a group of young men, among them A.B. Simpson, stood before the examining board. These elders were godly men, men of high principles, and they took their task seriously. Their special assignment was to lead the sheep through the gate that led to the pastures of higher learning, and at the same time keep the goats out.

When the day was over, this particular group of young men had all been accepted. The grizzled judges had given their nod of approval. All of a sudden they seemed human, too. Their warm handclasps betrayed the beat of heaven's drums to which both the young and old were marching.

Simpson was comfortable in the scholastic setting. He had time to spare which enabled him to fill empty pulpits on Sunday. That an 18-year-old farm boy should have such a remarkable talent for communicating the Gospel soon came to the attention of Presbyterians in other communities. It was not strange, therefore, that upon graduation four years later there were churchmen waiting to eagerly bid for his services.

Two churches already had extended calls to him. One was Knox Church, one of the most prestigious in Canada. The other was a small church in a little town in Dundes, Ontario. Which call should he accept? What was the will of God for him? Would not the smaller church keep him humble, poor, and spiritual?

Simpson arrived at his conclusion in a different way than most men. From his biographer, Dr. A.W. Tozer, we pick up his train of reasoning: "If I take the small church, it will demand little and I will give little. Result, stagnation; I will get soft and cease to grow. If I take the large church I will be compelled to rise to meet its heavier demands, and the very effort will develop the gifts of God which are in me. The small church may break me, but the large church will certainly help to make me."[3]

Having decided in favor of Knox Church, 21-year-old Simpson notified the leadership that he would accept their call.

On September 11 he delivered his first sermon. The following day he was ordained to the ministry, and the day after that he was married.

For the next eight years the young pastor fed and nurtured the flock at Knox Church. Those were good years. Seven hundred fifty members were added to the rolls, the church debt was retired, a number of prayer groups were started, and mission interest was kindled.

Then came a call from the Chestnut Church in Louisville, Kentucky. Larger than Knox Church, the salary offered was an astonishing $5000 per year. (To pastors of that day this was an enormous stipend. How could a clergyman, they reasoned, stay spiritual with such an income?) There were other inducements as well. There was unlimited opportunity for outreach for the enterprising pastor. This appealed to Simpson. And besides, the winters in the southland were not as harsh as in

Ontario. He accepted the call.

As a Canadian he had no axe to grind, neither with the Yankees nor the Rebs. Though the war had been over for nearly 10 years, the churches had not forgotten. The cities lying along the Mason-Dixon line had gone through difficult times, and efforts at revival had proved futile.

That is, until Simpson came.

Simpson had a vision of what God could do, so he called the church leaders together. He gave the pastors little opportunity to talk knowing this would only rekindle the fires of animosity and destroy whatever there was of the spirit of prayer. Instead, he set them to praying, and slowly the spirit of forgiveness and harmony began to take over.

The outgrowth of this reconciliation and intercession was a plan for a city-wide Union Evangelistic Campaign. The speaker would be the then well-known Major Whittle, assisted by the equally well-known singer P.P. Bliss. The campaign would be held in the public library hall in the heart of the city.

The effort was a great success. Upwards of 2,000 came each night and hundreds were converted.

The success of this gospel thrust went far beyond the expectations of Simpson. He had looked upon this effort as an "adventure in respectability," only to have his vision greatly enlarged, for the people had come from every strata of society with a substantial number from "below the tracks."

In all of this a change began to come over Simpson. A new dream emerged. It was the dream of world evangelization. There was just one problem—he was not ready. Before he could embark on such a venture, he would have to have a better view of himself and a greater concept of God.

As he listened to the gospel team of Whittle and Bliss and saw the magnificent response, he was thrilled. But why was his own heart in such turmoil? The man who had been so greatly used of God was still under construction. This time there lay before him—unknown to him—a much greater avenue of service.

It was not by chance, therefore, that he should have come in contact with Whittle and Bliss. These were friends of Moody, Sankey, F.B. Meyer, and others who had discovered the importance of the power of the Holy Spirit in their lives. And the Spirit was the key to their great success in evangelism.

Simpson could see that these men exuded spiritual vitality, and seeing and hearing them made him thirsty for a drink at the same well. But for a man so highly regarded and esteemed, the pathway to the well was a torturous one. Before God could add this spiritual dimension to his life, some subtracting had to be done.

For the first time Simpson began to see in his own soul what God had seen all along—pride. At the center of his soul and on the throne he saw a hideous sight—himself. Adding to his discomfort he saw sins and shortcomings, like demons, gleefully tormenting him. Surrounding this loomed an awful emptiness.

The days following the campaign were days of personal inventory and evaluation. The more Simpson looked at himself, the worse he looked. With that came the terrible feeling of being literally crushed. But this brought Simpson to his knees. In a final act of total renunciation and surrender, he threw himself on the mercy of God, ". . .not knowing," he says, "but that it would be death in the most literal sense before the morning light." Death it was, but it was death to the self-life. This 19th century Jacob became a new man, and in his own words, henceforth lived "a consecrated, crucified, and Christ-devoted life."

From that day on Simpson also had a new concept of the ministry. Like a soaring eagle he looked over the fences that separate people, and he beheld the multitudes yet uncared for. Before long the Sunday evening services of his congregation were moved to the much larger hall of the public library. Soon it was packed to capacity.

Now the daily newspapers got into the act. They gave Simpson front page coverage. Every Monday morning his sermon, in part or in whole, appeared in the Louisville papers.

Simpson had learned from Whittle and Bliss the value and growing power of good music. The combination of it and Simpson's powerful preaching brought even larger numbers to hear the Gospel of Christ.

The following winter the facilities of the public library hall were no longer available. "Why not try for Macauley's Theatre?" Simpson asked. This was one of the largest and most popular amusement centers in Louisville. The idea proved to be good for both the owner of the theater as well as Simpson, since the public did not frequent such a place on the Lord's day.

On opening night multitudes flocked to the theater for the evening service. The religious community was shocked. To think that the Gospel could have any value when dispensed from such premises was beyond the comprehension of many church-goers.

Meanwhile, much that had been going on in Simpson's personal life was in preparation for a world-wide ministry. God was continuing to mold and fashion His servant. Now, in spite of a new and much larger church building called Broadway Tabernacle, Simpson was restless. "What is it, Lord? What are you trying to tell me?" was the cry of his heart.

Then, in 1879, another call—this time from the 13th St. Church in New York City. He immediately resigned his Louisville charge and, at age 36, took up his new work.

Up until that point Simpson's journey of faith had taken him from one mountaintop to another. There had been the valleys, of course, but suddenly he stood at the base of what seemed to be an insurmountable mountain. His health was failing. A prominent physician had told him, "Your days are numbered."

The young man was confused and perplexed. What would become of his dreams? Were they only the delusions of an overwrought mind?

Facing what seemed certain death, Simpson heard of the

teaching about the fullness of the Holy Spirit and how it had enlivened many an individual and church fellowship. There also was talk about praying for the sick and seeing people restored to health. Simpson probably would not have given the idea the time of day, had it not been for his own desperate need.

Supernatural phenomenon, where leadership is absent, often is followed by abuses which bring a legitimate truth into disrepute. However, Simpson's good fortune was to learn of Dr. Charles Cullis, a Boston physician, well respected among his peers and head of a tuberculosis sanitarium in Boston. This godly man, in addition to treating patients, had begun to pray for them as well. His success was so phenomenal that he abandoned the use of medicine and resorted to prayer alone for his patients' deliverance. His unusual success soon propelled him into full time Christian service of preaching and praying for the sick.

At Old Orchard, Maine, a well-known summer resort and conference ground, Simpson heard Cullis speak. But it was not the speaker that impressed him as much as the testimonies of those who had been healed.

Many persons shared how they had been restored by the power of God and by faith. Just as they had trusted Christ for salvation, so now they had trusted Him for healing.

Whatever he thought about the doctrine of healing as being a valid teaching in the Word of God, Simpson could not ignore the facts: these people had been ill, but now they were well.

Simpson went to the Word of God for his final authority. His reading and studying fed those smoldering embers of hope. One day on a walk through a wooded area, he dropped to his knees by a fallen log. The power of Christ came upon him. His ailing heart was healed instantly.

Simpson did not remain long at the 13th Street Presbyterian Church. The world now was his parish. He did not start a new church, but began to bring Christians together in great rallies to share his missionary vision with them. The meetings were held Sunday afternoons so as not to conflict with the regular church services.

Attendance at the first service was small, and only a handful were present for the mid-week prayer meeting in the Simpson home. But, like a rolling snowball, the momentum increased. Sinners were being saved, others found healing for their bodies, and still others sought and found power to live the Christian life. Converts visited the hospitals, jails, and missions every week. In a very poor part of town a building had been refurbished where meals could be obtained without charge. Simpson's parishioners provided the food. The local inhabitants provided the name. . ."Hell's Kitchen."

The Gospel Tabernacle, as it came to be called, consisted of a large auditorium and three smaller chapels. The education building housed the training institute, a bookstore, a nursing home and a Christian hotel.

The center of the enterprise, however, was the pulpit of the Gospel Tabernacle. Simpson was, of course, the guiding spirit. He was one of the outstanding preachers of his day, but he wanted his people to know and hear the voice of God through other vessels as well. In this he was singularly successful. For more than a quarter of a century the leading pastors and missionaries of the world converged there.

Under his leadership two missionary organizations which he had helped start were merged into one, and came to be known as "The Christian and Missionary Alliance." The work continued to grow both at home and abroad. He had not planned that it take on the appearance of a denomination. Therefore, the leaders were not called pastors but superintendents. However, they had to face up to the fact that the converts wanted to be baptized. They wanted the Lord's Supper. They wanted a church home for their families and wanted a place from which they could be married and buried.

Slowly the denominational framework came into view.

The doctrinal position of the Pentecostal movement, which began in the early part of the century, was very close to that of Simpson. However, there was one truth with which he did not agree. This was that speaking in tongues is the evidence of the baptism of the Holy Spirit. He finally made his position clear in a public manifesto in which he spelled out his position. As a result a number of churches under the Christian and Missionary Alliance banner pulled out of the society. This came as a severe blow to the church and no doubt to Simpson, too. However, he continued to lead the work that God had given him, and after a few years it became stronger than ever.

Simpson was 76 when he was called home. He could confidently say he had kept the faith. His lifelong objectives had been the same. "It is," said he, "to hold up Jesus in His fullness, 'the same yesterday, today and forever.' It is to lead God's spiritually hungry children to know their full inheritance of privilege and blessing for spirit, soul, and body. It is to encourage and incite the people of God to do the neglected work of their age and time among the unchurched classes at home and the perishing heathen abroad." The summary of his theology is further condensed in the slogan of the Christian and Missionary Alliance, "Christ our Savior, Sanctifier, Healer and Coming King."

The pilgrimage of his interior life is beautifully set forth in his well-known poem entitled "Himself":

Once it was the blessing, now it is the Lord;
Once it was the feeling, now it is His Word;
Once His gifts I wanted, now the Giver own;
Once I sought for healing, now Himself alone.

Once 'twas painful trying, now 'tis perfect trust;
Once a half salvation, now the uttermost;
Once 'twas ceaseless holding, now He holds me fast;

Once 'twas constant drifting, now my anchor's cast.

Once 'twas busy planning, now 'tis trustful prayer;
Once 'twas anxious caring, now He has the care;
Once 'twas what I wanted, now what Jesus says;
Once 'twas constant asking, now 'tis ceaseless praise.

Once it was my working, His it hence shall be;
Once I tried to use Him, now He uses me;
Once the power I wanted, now the Mighty One;
Once for self I labored, now for Him alone. . .

[1]A.W. Tozer, *Wingspread*, pg. 17.
[2]*Ibid.*, p. 18.
[3]Tozer, p. 39.

2

Henry Clay Morrison (1857-1942)

Methodist

The audience sat spellbound as the greatest pulpit orator of the South introduced the silver-tongued patriot of American politics, William Jennings Bryan. Bryan responded, "Morrison, I find where I have made a big mistake. I should have remained at home during my campaigns for president and engaged you to go up and down the land to represent me. I should certainly have been elected."[1]

Henry Clay Morrison came from the bluegrass country. He was born November 10, 1857, just three years before the beginning of the Civil War. His maternal grandfather was the first Methodist class leader in Kentucky. He was a wealthy man with large land holdings and the owner of a considerable number of slaves, but every day the heads of his black families would meet at the "big house" for prayer at the family altar.

His paternal grandfather was William (Uncle Billy) Morrison, who lived in Barren County. He is described as "quaint, quiet, thoughtful, stern, although in his way exceedingly kind." Later the grandson was to offer this tribute: "My grandfather was my ideal of all human excellencies and greatness."

Henry Clay, or "Bud" as he came to be called, was raised by his paternal grandparents. His parents, as newlyweds, had settled in a beautiful old home on the "borderland of the richest and most prosperous section to be found in America," but tragedy struck early. First Morrison's mother fell ill and died. Only months later his father was killed in one of the early battles of the Civil War. Morrison and a sister several years older went to live with their grandparents and an aunt.

His grandfather's house proved a good place for young Morrison to grow up. Like most farmboys, he was doing a man's job before he was in his teens. But it wasn't all work. There was play and relaxation, too. A rather common sight was the barefoot boy in his straw hat, pole in one hand and a can of worms in the other, on his way to his favorite fishing hole. When fall came he headed for the "bluffs and thickets." He was the proud owner of a single barrel shotgun, and with his dog at his side he wiled away many a Saturday afternoon in search of a fox, 'coon or an opossum.

Morrison was fortunate his community had many godly men and women who were concerned about the spiritual welfare of others. They left their imprint upon Morrison.

Then there was the circuit rider, the Rev. James M. Phillips. In a "revival" at the Boyds Creek meeting house, Morrison's sister Emily and most of his boyhood associates were converted. But not Morrison. He was under deep conviction because of his sins, but no one invited him to come forward. In later years in his revival work he remembered some of those scenes from his boyhood. The terrible agony of his friends as they struggled at the altar gave him a conception of the wretchedness of sin which he never forgot.

There were other men who helped make up the moral and spiritual conscience of the community. William Snoody was the Sunday School superintendent. He was a man, people said, who "enjoyed full salvation." Then there was another local Methodist preacher and four Baptist ministers. These were men of limited education, but they knew God. They presented the Bible plan of salvation clearly, and for good measure they preached on judgment and eternal punishment as well. In later years Morrison, with deep gratitude, said, "I shall always feel thankful that in early childhood I heard these men preach. There was nothing in their sermons to make one laugh. With solemn faces, uplifted hands and in thundering tones they cried out to men to repent or perish."

Since the Methodist pastors were moved from year to year, there was some question whether Phillips would be back. This concerned the young boy. He remembered so well the "revival" of the previous year when so many of his friends had been saved, so he made a covenant with God: If Phillips was reassigned to the same circuit for the following year, he would seek God.

Christmas week came, and with it revival meetings. Now 13, Morrison decided to sit near the aisle so that if anyone wanted to speak to him about his soul he would have easy access to him. Then, too, he would be as close to the altar rail as possible.

At the close of the first service the invitation was given. But no one invited him to the altar. He describes the struggle:

It seemed as if I were riveted to the spot; I felt as if the power of locomotion had left me. It seemed for a time that my will lost power over my feet, and I could not make them move. The spell of the tempter was on me, but leaning forward I broke away. The first step taken, the next was easy, and I almost ran to the altar.[2]

But when Morrison arrived at the altar, the anticipated release and freedom did not come. What was wrong? Later he realized he was counting on counterfeit currency with which to purchase the favors of God. First of all, he reasoned he was

29

not as bad as some of the other boys in the community. Then, he was an orphan boy, which would undoubtedly appeal to God's compassion. But ". . .instead of peace," he tells us, a "heavy load seemed settling down on my heart."

Instead of feeling better after coming to the altar rail, he felt worse. But, without knowing it, he was standing on the threshold of a new day. An important conclusion had taken shape in his mind: "Up to this time I feared I might be lost; now I clearly saw that I was lost."

But God's release was at hand. It came in the form of a man who, in a tender voice, said, "Bud, God is not mad at you. . .God loves you." Then he quoted John 3:16. In an instant the young seeker was on his feet praising God.

During this time he was to learn some valuable lessons that were to stand him in good stead when his turn came to lead men into the kingdom. He came to have little sympathy with the altar worker who would instruct the seeker to just "take it by faith" or "confess Christ." He came to appreciate the deep wisdom of the elders who did not interfere, but allowed the Spirit of God to have His day in court.

Morrison left his grandfather's farm and for some years lived with a half brother in another county. This was fortunate for him. He had some opportunity to attend school, and the community was less class-conscious. The young man was only a farm hand, and this must have been, in the eyes of a blue blood, only a notch above a slave. But this community was different. The lines of class distinction were not so pronounced. They received him for what he was, and he was happy.

Yet he had a burden. He had carried it for some time, but never shared it with anyone. It was a call to Christian service. But how could a farm boy, with limited education, aspire to preach the Gospel? He prayed and pondered over this for weeks. God's answer to his prayer came about in a most interesting way.

The people of the village of Perryville and the surrounding

community had encouraged the formation of a debating society. In this way many of the current issues were discussed. This was the outlet that young Morrison needed. In a rather graphic way he tells us what transpired:

Often I worked all day, and prepared my speech between the handles of the plow; and after supper, cleaned up, walked to town, and participated in the debates, getting home at a very late hour. The excitement of public speaking so exhilarated me that my whole body seemed charged with energy, and although we lived four miles out of town I took short cuts and made it a little less, but seemed to feel no fatigue whatever.[3]

The local Methodist pastor viewed with more than average interest this budding public speaker. As their friendship ripened, the young man confided for the first time the secret of his call to the ministry. The pastor, of course, was pleased.

"He gave me every possible encouragement," said Morrison. "He furnished me with books, had me often to the parsonage and licensed me to exhort, and he had me speak to his people from time to time."

He preached his first sermon at Johnson's Chapel on the banks of the Rolling Fork river in Casey County, Kentucky. The results were gratifying. He decided to hold a service in his home town of Perryville, where he had gained some reputation as a debater. A single announcement was enough to pack the house, but the results were catastrophic. After announcing his text he lost his composure. All he could say was "God has called me to preach." Then silence. Again he repeated, "The God of Abraham, Isaac and Jacob has called me to preach." Again more silence. Finally he broke into tears as he repeated the text, "Repent, for the kingdom of heaven is at hand."

By this time the congregation was weeping with him. There was considerable relief when he finally said "amen" and sat down. It was a sobering moment for the young prodigy who had envisioned himself as already halfway to the stars, but it was a blessing in disguise, for it was one of his early lessons in humility. He would learn that if inroads were going to be made into the enemy's kingdom, it would be not by human might and power, but by the power of God.

Before many months had passed he gave up his farm work and joined the pastor who had, by now, been transferred to another part of the state. The next step was a circuit of his own. . .a five-point preaching circuit touching three counties. At last he was a part of that probing army of God's men who were out on the frontier, encouraging the saints and ferreting out the sinners.

Morrison rose rapidly in the ranks of the circuit riders. His ability as a preacher was heralded abroad, and larger churches were-competing with each other for his services.

Then came an assignment to Stanford, a large and prestigious call. This was the county seat with a population of 3,000. Among his parishioners were many professional people.

In this congregation was one whom he called an "elect lady." He would remember her always. "She was," he said, "a patient, pale little maiden enjoying 'full salvation.' " But in years to come he often marveled that this experience she possessed, and which certain others sought after, had eluded him.

The young minister felt keenly his lack of formal education, so he enrolled at Vanderbilt University in Nashville, Tennessee. Nashville was the "Athens of the South" and the center of southern Methodism. The university had been founded by the Methodists 30 years before, and as yet was untouched by higher criticism.

After his year at Vanderbilt he returned to the pastoral ministry. He was now about 28 years old. Some of the leading churches continued to "pull" for him to be their pastor. There was 11th St., Covington, Highlands, Danville, Frankfurt. Each was a promotion.

In the midst of all his success he developed a mysterious burden. The proud pulpit orator, the popular and dressy man about town, was fighting an inner battle he hardly understood. The peace of heart that he proclaimed to others he did not himself possess. In addition, he confessed to an "impetuous temper" and lack of power in Christian service.

Ministry under these circumstances became increasingly more difficult. Meanwhile, he began to recall certain people whom he had ignored up to this time. They spoke in glowing terms of a "higher life," "full salvation," "entire sanctification," being "sanctified," and the "Pentecostal blessing." What did they mean? He recalled to mind Mary McAfee in his Stanford congregation. Though he had not understood her, he could not forget her. Then there was the Rev. W.B. Godby, of the Kentucky conference, who professed entire sanctification. A noted evangelist by the name of Barnes talked about the "higher life," and professed to be "sanctified." Then there was the Rev. H.B. Cockrill, a close associate, who became interested and finally came into the "Pentecostal blessing."

Morrison was dining one day when a letter was delivered to him. It was from Cockrill. In it he rehearsed how he had entered into his pentecost. In that moment Morrison saw the doctrine was meant for him. Later in the day he went to his room, expecting to be "sanctified wholly."

He was not disappointed, but his encounter with the Spirit of God was more than he had bargained for. On entering the room his limbs gave way and he sagged to the sofa. A companion, Dr. Young, greatly alarmed, caught him in his arms as he was falling and tried to arouse him. Morrison said later that the experience lasted only a few moments, but as he was regaining the use of his limbs and his mind was beginning to clear a great ball of liquid fire seemed to descend and strike him in the face and dissolve and enter into him. In a moment he was on his feet and with typical Methodist enthusiasm shouted, "Glory to God!" Young, who had thought moments before that his friend was dying, now sat spellbound as he watched this exuberant Methodist preacher extol the mercy of God, shouting, "The Lord did it!"

Then a strange thing happened. Not being willing to testify to the blessing because of the fear of man, he lost it. For months he lived with only a memory, and he said later, "I had a foretaste of what it would be to be separated from Him forever."

In his misery he sought help from a Presbyterian minister, Dr. McKee, a professor of theology. Here he was given some much-needed instruction and encouragement. Said McKee, "My young brother, the Lord has not forsaken you, but is leading you into what John Wesley called 'Christian perfection,'" the Baptists call it the 'rest of faith,' the Presbyterians call it the 'higher life' or the 'fullness of the Spirit.'"[4]

That day the young preacher had to be assisted to his quarters. Loss of sleep and fasting had left him exhausted. The blessing returned, but, "dreading the consequences of telling his cultured and fastidious congregation that God had sanctified him, the blessed assurance departed from him a second time. This meant many more days and nights of bitter struggle before he became rooted and grounded in the faith."[5]

This proud and gifted man, however, at last became the humble servant God intended him to be. Soon he was declaring to everyone the power of Jesus' blood to sanctify the soul. It was not too soon. The enemy had been, for some time, undermining the foundations of Methodism. Satan had, to a great extent, stifled the voices for entire sanctification, and now his underlings were worming their way into the pulpit and proclaiming "another gospel" (Galatians 1:6).

During his Danville pastorate he met and married Laura

Band, and to this union were added two boys and a girl. From Danville he was sent to Frankfurt, Kentucky. This was a much larger charge. While there he also had the privilege of serving as chaplain of the Senate and the House of Representatives.

The churches continued vying for his services, but the evangelistic field was beckoning him, too. After about two years in Frankfurt he resigned his church and launched out into a full time evangelistic career.

The office of the evangelist had fallen on hard times, even in the Methodist church. It was no longer held in the high esteem it had once enjoyed. Without salary or church backing he began to hold protracted services in response to many invitations. Multitudes came. . .to brush arbors, country churches, and camp meetings. They knelt, wept, repented, and consecrated themselves to God who in turn met them, saved them, and filled them with His Holy Spirit. The "new evangelism" had taken root. But the "new" was only the old Methodism of yesteryears. This was what the forefathers had enjoyed and proclaimed. They had called it "entire sanctification."

Morrison felt his limitations. He could, after all, be in only one place at a time. So during one of his campaigns he decided to publish a small newspaper to champion the cause of the deeper life.

The first issue came off the press about the year 1890. It was called *The Old Methodist*, consisted of four pages and went to 500 homes.

The Methodist leadership did not take it seriously at first. To them it was a joke. But the "joke" grew. In time it became *The Kentucky Methodist* and still later evolved into its final form as *The Pentecostal Herald*, reaching into 100,000 homes. As an overseas periodical it reached out to more people than any other paper of its kind.

But with the success of his publication and his evangelistic ministry came years of conflict. . .of "priestly hate and ecclesiastical inquisition."

Opposition was formidable. In the annual district and quarterly conferences his work was ridiculed and opposed. He was branded as a heretic and accused of being a fanatic and disturber of the peace.

The climax came when Morrison was put on trial and expelled from the ministry of the Methodist Episcopal church. To the credit of the men of this "ecclesiastical machinery," on seeing what they had obviously blundered, they shortly reversed themselves and restored Morrison to this former place in the church.

For more than a quarter of a century Morrison traversed the land from coast to coast and around the world. Large crowds gathered to hear him, and he was considered the greatest pulpit orator of the South. But his joy in Christian service was tempered by burdens and sorrows. For many years *The Pentecostal Herald* did not pay its way, and all too often the offerings were less than adequate. But somehow the publications survived and so did Morrison.

Then there were the more personal and intimate trials. His first wife died, leaving him with three small children. Then his second wife, who had borne five children, also died while the children were still young.

Time has a way of healing rifts and hurts. The most misunderstood man in Methodism came to be accepted and honored by his fellow men. They might not agree with him, but they had to respect him.

He was in a camp meeting in Indiana when a message was handed him: "Will you accept the presidency of Asbury College?" At first he declined, but when he learned that the only other option for the board of directors was to sell the school to pay off its indebtedness, he yielded and agreed to serve.

It was a stupendous undertaking, and it was generally agreed that Morrison was the only man who could save the school.

When he began there were no adequate buildings, no faculty, no money, and no standing.

In his favor, Morrison was well known, the people trusted him, and his converts were everywhere. Soon students came from almost every state in the Union, as well as from many foreign countries. In a matter of just a few years the college was back on a sound financial basis, buildings were restored, furniture had been added, and the faculty had been upgraded. The school had earned an equal accreditation with other colleges in the state.

What was of greatest importance was that Henry Clay Morrison, in the providence of God, had saved and restored an institution that would continue to herald forth the great truth of Methodism, namely, the doctrine of entire sanctification.

[1]C.F. Wimberly, *A Biography of Henry Clay Morrison*, pg. 128.
[2]Wimberly, p. 57.
[3]Wimberly, p. 70.
[4]Wimberly, p. 98.
[5]Wimberly, p. 98.

Charles G. Trumbull (1872-1941)

Presbyterian

"**I** can never forget," said the speaker, "the 14th day of August, 1910, when the scales dropped from my eyes and I saw that Christ was my life. Christ was my victory." This was a Christian leader, well known through his column in his own prestigious journal, the *Sunday School Times*, baring his heart, confessing his defeat, but now sharing how he emerged from the dark tunnel of defeat into the glorious sunshine of God's provision. Candidly he acknowledged that at the age of 38 he had come to the end of his spiritual resources and had not known what to do. The recital of his bitter dilemma and consequent discovery held the attention of everyone.

Dr. Charles G. Trumbull explained that he had made a public profession of faith at the age of 13, and had been an active Christian all of his adult life. But in later years the gnawing feeling grew that all was not well. No amount of extra Christian activity had assuaged that feeling. Not even his column in the *Sunday School Times* on the deity of Christ could satisfy his aching heart. What was the difficulty? He did not know. But from various directions, and through different men, God seemed to be saying, "There is yet more." How could that be? Was he not one of the leaders in the evangelical world of that day? Could there be a concept of Christ that he did not understand? Hardly—or so he thought.

Many hours he spent huddling with his conscience, for he was a troubled and depressed man. In recounting this period in his life, Trumbull said, "I think I am correct when I say that I have known more than most men know about failure, about betrayals and dishonorings of Christ, about disobedience to heavenly visions, about conscious fallings-short of that which I saw other men attaining, and which I knew Christ was expecting of me."

He summarized the failures of the past in terms of great fluctuations in his spiritual life. At times he would be on the mountain-top, then would come the valley. There also was the matter of failure before besetting sins. In certain areas he was fighting a losing battle. He was mystified by this. The Bible seemed to offer victory, but up to that time it had escaped him. Finally, there was the lack of dynamic spiritual power that could work miracles and change the lives of others. This, he felt, was the need of the hour. And the Scriptures and the lives of certain believers past and present seemed to support such a possibility. In fact, he became convinced that he had come far short of the real thing, and what he had was hardly worth exporting.

Trumbull, however, did not quit. But neither could he find the opening in the forest that led to the meadow. God places a premium on despair, for He knows that that is the gateway to a better life. It is there that a man ceases to expect anything from himself, and in that moment he discovers that his sufficiency is to be found in God.

One day Trumbull heard a sermon on Ephesians 4:13-14, "Unto the building up of the Body of Christ: till we all attain unto the unity of the faith and the knowledge of the Son of God, unto a full grown man, unto the measure of the stature of the fullness of Christ."

Trumbull was perplexed. Amazed. Bewildered. He couldn't follow him. The preacher was unfolding Christ in an utterly unknown way. Later he read another sermon by this same man on "Paul's conception of the Lord Jesus Christ." Slowly he realized that, although he was a Christian, he did not know the Christ Paul was talking about.

One day he met another minister, one of those choice men who always seemed to spread the sunshine of God's love.

From this man he obtained a ray of hope. It was a truth that he had often seen in the Word of God but it had never penetrated his heart. It was the truth of the daily and continual presence of the Lord Jesus in his life. It was a fact, independent of his feelings or his deserts. The contemplation of this truth, said the minister, had become a part of his life and Jesus was ever the home of his thoughts.

Trumbull was in Scotland at the time, attending the World Missionary Conference, when he saw that a man whose writings had been a great help to him was speaking on Sunday afternoon. The subject intrigued Trumbull. He was to speak on the resources of the Christian life. Perhaps he would get some help, perhaps some keys to Christian victory would be shared.

Eagerly he awaited the afternoon session. But what a bombshell! When God's artillery man pulled the lanyard, there was but one shot and it was enough. The words of the opening salvo were these: "The resources of the Christian life, my friends, are just Jesus Christ." That was all.

The projectile may have missed many, but it went right to the heart of Trumbull. His heart was now prepared for further revelation. As the speaker unfolded Jesus Christ, Trumbull thought, "This is what all these other men have been saying." He had not come to the crest of the hill where he could view the beautiful panoramic view below, but he was near.

It was the month of June. The pastor's text for the Sunday evening was Philippians 1:21, "To me to Live is Christ." Here again was a man unfolding Jesus Christ like those other men he had been hearing.

By now Trumbull was convinced that what they were saying was for real, but he himself could see only the faintest glimmer. . .no more. His need and eagerness prompted him to ask the pastor if he might take the manuscript with him and study it. Permission was gladly granted. A couple of months later another crisis loomed on the horizon.

Trumbull was speaking at a young people's missionary conference which required much preparation. However, emotionally and spiritually he did not feel up to the task before him. For weeks he had been depressed and had been going through a period of spiritual letdowns with the consequent failure and defeat which so often follows.

The speaker for the opening session was a missionary bishop who spoke on "The Water of Life." Again, the prominent note through the entire sermon was of the sufficiency of Christ for man's every need. Man had not been sparingly provided for, as many believers seemed to think and live, but on the contrary, provision had been made for abundant living. . .for a victorious life. Jesus had said, "He that believeth on me from within him shall flow rivers of living water." He went on to contrast the creaking, squeaking irrigation water wheel of India. But God's plan was not the Christian life of mere existence, but rather an abundant, radiant life in which people could see Jesus.

The next morning he "prayed it out with God." By now it was obvious that these men he had been hearing had a concept of Christ that he did not have. He prayed for his eyes to be opened that he might see what his heart was crying for. Before him was the sermon he had heard, "To Me to Live is Christ." He studied it. He prayed over it. Suddenly the scales fell from his eyes. He saw the truth of the indwelling Christ.

But it was not an emotional burst that shook his religious bearings. This staid Presbyterian would have resisted any kind of physical or emotional excess. Rather it was the eye-opening experience of a new revelation, but only new to him. After all, the indwelling presence of God in His people was not new. Now he could understand Paul, when he was addressing the learned Athenians on Mars Hill, saying, "In Him we live and move and have our being" (Acts 17:28).

Out of the shadows trooped a host of other Bible texts. There was John 7:37-39, Ephesians 3:14-21 and Philippians 1:21. All of these Scriptures spoke of a Christ who indwelt His people. So *this* was the victorious life that had eluded him all these years. Now he not only had a Savior from the penalty of sin but a Savior who had come to give him the needed power for Christian life and service. Now he discovered that he did not have to wait for victory until he got to heaven. It was for the here and now.

Trumbull was never the same again. He had a long and fruitful ministry as the editor of the *Sunday School Times*. He exemplified the Christian life. He was, "friendly, approachable, courteous, always considerate and fair with those with whom he had to disagree. . ." He was further described as a buoyant, joyous, earnest, unassuming, spirit-filled Christian journalist and leader."

In 1910, the year following his new experience with God he was asked to address The National Convention of the Presbyterian Brotherhood of America. The theme of his message was, "The Life That Wins." "There is only one life that wins," he said, "and that's the life of Jesus Christ. Every man may have that life; every man may live that life." Then he went on to give his testimony of how he had been lifted from the depths of despair to a place of joy, peace, and constant victory.

Trumbull never tired of bringing the message of the life of victory. He said it was obtained but never attained—a gift requiring no price. If one had to work for it, it was not the real thing. One of his favorite texts was Romans 6:14: "Sin shall not have dominion over you: for ye are not under law but under grace." His comment was, "Ye are not under law which says do, but under grace that says done."

Trumbull might have called his encounter with God by some other name if his church background (Presbyterian) and circumstances had been different. Instead, he used language nearest at hand, language that was familiar to him. To him this deeper encounter with God would always be called "the victorious Christian life." No one spelled it out better than he did. It was a work of God, not man. It was God's job to save man and make him holy. Man's part was to receive and trust. He once said, "I speak with deep feeling as to this because I lived to be nearly 40 years old, never knowing what real victory was."

4

William Booth (1829-1912)

Salvation Army

They have girded the world with a network of outposts. For more than 100 years they have been conveyors of kindness and good news to the legions of the lost. They have been among the most disciplined workers in Christian service. They are called "soldiers." With sword in hand (the Bible) they have courageously invaded the enemy's domain and challenged the usurper. Thereupon these enclaves of the dead would grudgingly relinquish their prey one at a time as the victims were baited by the army's creed, "soup, soap, and salvation."

The Salvation Army came to birth in a time of great need. England, the mightiest and wealthiest nation in the world, was the hub of great maritime activity. Raw materials from every corner of the British empire poured into its ports daily. England had responded by becoming an industrial nation, turning out the finished products for the markets of the world. But in the process it had dislocated many of its people. They had fled the countryside and farmlands to work in the cities.

In the cities they were confronted with a way of life for which they were not prepared. The long working hours, poor pay, and large families in squalid quarters produced an incredible situation. The Thames River was so polluted it was called the "great stink." As it meandered through London it would gather to its bosom the water from 370 sewers. Cholera had struck the city three times since 1832, and next year it would strike again.

In these crowded conditions little or no provision had been made for the social and spiritual life of the people. There were no community halls and few, if any, churches. But there were pubs. . .thousands of them. Every fifth door leading to the street was an invitation to come in, relax, and forget your troubles. But the price was high. It would be a man's wages, his character, and his life. Hanging in the balance would be a wife and children. The women of the street only added to the misery.

But one day a harbinger of better days to come approached this human jungle. It came in the form of a man from England's midlands. The scrawny six footer had never seen the likes of this before. The more he saw the more he wanted to see. He wondered: How big was London's open sore? How many unfortunates were clasped in its embrace? One could hardly say that the long strides of this man of God were eating up the 2,000 miles of London's streets, but before the day was over he had seen a city with a horrendous need, and in the process he had heard that faint but distinct call, "Who will go for us?" He, like Isaiah, had appropriately answered, "Here am I, send me" (Isaiah 6:8).

It was near midnight when William Booth arrived home after his tour of London's streets. Though bone tired from his day's journey, his eyes hone as he triumphantly announced to his wife Catherine, "Darling, I have found my destiny!" Excitedly he shared with her what he had seen and heard. It was God's call. He was sure. His wife was supportive but concerned. They

45

had met and married when they were both 23. Now, 13 years and six children later, they would be living in London's ghetto with no visible means of support. How would they fare?

Booth had found the Lord under the ministry of the Methodists when he was about 15. From that time on he had been eager to serve God, but his job as an apprentice in a pawnbroker's shop left little time for attendance at services, much less doing any kind of Christian work. But the boy was strong, resourceful and determined. His strong will had earned him the dubious nickname of "Willful Will." He would find a way.

An incident from those early days could have curbed his Christian witness, but it turned out otherwise. Having become a Christian there were now certain principles that the Lord's people considered inviolate. Working on Sunday was a case in point. Sunday was the Lord's day—a time of rest, spiritual refreshment and labor of another kind. When Booth announced to Mr. Eames, his employer, that he would no longer be able to work on Sunday the response was curt and to the point: You'll work with the rest of us until we shut up shop or you can leave. So Booth left. To all outward appearances it was a foolhardy decision, for there were large numbers of people unemployed. Besides, he had his widowed mother to support. But young Booth had been the pawnbroker's best employee and now he was sorely missed. A few days later he was called back to work with the concession that he would not have to work on Sunday.

He was 19 when the term of his apprenticeship expired. During that time he had actively pursued the Christian ministry as time allowed. The Methodists had been good to him. Under their ministry he had found God. They were the ones who had encouraged him in his lay activity and appointed him a local preacher at 17.

However, there was something confining about Methodist church life. The people had become staid and satisfied. This reality came into full focus one Sunday at Broadstreet Chapel when Booth herded "a shabby contingent" of the poor into the main sanctuary. What should have been an occasion for rejoicing was instead met with the cold stare of the more proper folk. The problem was Methodism had become "respectable." They were no longer the shouting Methodists of yesteryear.

It was not strange, therefore, that when the service was over Booth was ushered into the presence of the pastor and deacons. The instructions were unmistakable and to the point: In the future he would have to bring his ragtag congregation in by the side door where accommodations were provided for the likes of such. It was a screened off and segregated area. There were only benches to sit on, with no backs or cushions. They could not see the pulpit, but neither could anyone see them.

This growing chasm between the underprivileged and the more affluent did not go unnoticed by some of the leaders in the Methodist church. But their agitation for reform had thus far been unproductive.

Finally, the inevitable happened. There was a split. The churches that were for reform seceded from the parent body, and ministers with similar leanings were either dismissed or dropped from the rolls. Among them was Booth. But he was not unemployed for long. Soon he was the pastor of one of the chapels in London where he ministered with considerable success.

But this man had more than a pastor's heart. The mantle of the evangelist was also upon him. Unable to persuade his superiors to release him for full-time evangelism, he resigned from the Methodist New Connection. He would go it alone, independent of any existing organization.

The time was no doubt right for such a step of faith. God had readied His vessel and now He was opening the door. Shortly before this time Booth and his wife had both been led into a deeper Christian experience with God. They had both been diligent students of the writings of John Wesley and had accepted his views on the subject of sanctification and holiness. They believed with Wesley that holiness or a holy life was possible for the here and now.

But reaching this plateau of Christian experience had not been easy. Like most seekers they began by struggling to achieve instead of resting and accepting from God's hand what had already been provided. Booth seems to have entered into this experience first, for we see him attempting to assist his wife, who was struggling and grappling with unbelief.

By now Catherine's personal need for holiness had become an unbearable burden. She had struggled throughout the day, seeking and praying, but could find no rest. In the evening her husband joined her. She began to see that her problem was her unbelief. Her husband gently challenged her, "Didn't you lay all on the altar?" She replied that she thought she had. Slowly the blade of faith began to show itself through the crusty ground of unbelief. A verse of Scripture was given her, "Now are ye clean through the Word I have spoken unto you." The woman who had struggled to find holiness by works now found it was by faith. What was at first a faint realization of a wonderful truth grew in her heart so that it became one of the major themes of her preaching and teaching in days to come.

Launching out into an independent ministry is never easy. For the Booths there was a long period of testing. Then came a request for services in Cornwall. A spiritual awakening began to stir the people. Soon no building was large enough so they did the only thing they could do. They held open-air meetings with great success.

Around the year 1865 their labors took a new direction. One morning while in a conference, Booth's oldest son, Bramwell, then 22, took note of a statement in the mission's annual report that angered him. "The Christian Mission," so read the report, "under the superintendance of the Rev. William Booth is a voluntary army. . ."

"Volunteer!" he exclaimed, "I am a regular or not at all."

Booth, under the inspiration of the moment, borrowed a pen, crossed out volunteer and replaced it with the word "salvation." Thus was born "The Salvation Army." In a sense it could be said that the army began with one family. And what a family it was. Someone has said that the "General" and Mrs. Booth raised the most efficient family for God the world has ever known. This is no doubt an overstatement, but that this one was unique in terms of gifts and Christian commitment, there is no question.

Booth was supported by his gifted and talented wife. She was first of all an unusual mother. The children, almost from infancy, were made aware of their high calling. "The world is waiting for you," she would whisper in the child's ear as she rocked him to sleep. In the same breath she might serve notice on the devil, "I am not raising any children for you." Once she reminded her daughter Kate, "You are not in this world for yourself. The world is waiting for you." Booth and his wife had lived the Christian life for all to see. Their daughter, Evangeline, once replied, "My parents did not have to say anything to me about Christianity. I saw it in action."

When other mothers wondered how such a large family had never experienced the death of any of its children, Catherine would reply, "Perhaps because I gave them so fully to God that He did not think it necessary to take them away from me."

Catherine was a great evangelist in her own right. Intelligent, compassionate and articulate, she would hold her large audiences spellbound as she pleaded the cause of God. Combined with her oratorical powers was that rare understanding of the human heart. Having peered into the windows of their souls she was once heard to say, "I looked into their eyes and they were veritable cesspools of iniquity."

Gifted as she was, however, Catherine did not rely on this for success in the ministry. Here she was true as steel to her Master. She knew that apart from the anointing of God there could be no lasting results.

The Salvation Army became a unique institution. Booth had been a student of Wellington and Napoleon. This inspired him to draft a handbook entitled *Orders and Regulations for the Salvation Army*. This was based largely on Field Marshall Sir Garnet Wolseley's *Field Pocket Book for Auxiliary Forces*. Now the Army had a name, a uniform and a manual. Catherine later designed the "Hallelujah Bonnet" and other adaptations followed. Church vocabulary was too musty; it had to be altered. Their official publication entitled *The Christian Mission* became *The War Cry*. The annual conference became a "War Congress." The Mission house became a "citadel" or a "fort." When you knelt to pray it was "knee drill." "Fire a volley" was the signal for a hallelujah shout. "Fix bayonets" meant you raised your right hand in public declaration. In everyday army life old soldiers fade away and die. Not so in this Army. These soldiers were promoted to glory.

With all this novelty in Christian work, the final key to success was yet to be uncovered. They had felt for some time that something was missing, but what was it?

The missing ingredient was discovered by accident. The Army had been troubled by hooligans who had abused its members in the street services. Because of this continual maltreatment a man by the name of Charles Fry approached Booth one day and offered the services of himself and his three sons as bodyguards. This offer was gratefully accepted. It was only an afterthought that made them bring their musical instruments. The father was a musician and choir leader. He also played the coronet. His sons played brass instruments. All of a sudden the street meeting became a lively affair as these men accompanied the singing with their instruments. Interest mounted rapidly.

Music, however, like everything else, came under scrutiny and change. They were known for taking secular tunes and adding Christian lyrics. For instance, the song, "Joy, Freedom, Peace and Ceaseless Blessing" was now sung to the tune of

"Old Folks at Home." The Scottish folk loved to sing "Storm the Forts of Darkness, Bring Them Down," probably because they had first known, "Here's to Good Old Whiskey." It is doubtful that such changes could have been accomplished in a traditional church setting. To be sure the melody of Luther's "Ein feste Burg" (A Mighty Fortress) came from the German tavern, but not many people know that.

Booth learned early that, "It is in the interest of the Army to be in the columns of the newspaper as often as possible." But here, too, they were to learn that the announcement of an impending event was not necessarily the key to bring the people out. It could be *how* it was said. On one occasion two ladies were sent to one of the cities for special service. The handbill announcing their arrival originally referred to them as "two lady preachers," but the printer felt that this lacked punch. Instead he called the ladies "Hallelujah Lasses." Booth was shocked, but after a few days the printer was vindicated, for no building in Tynside could contain the crowds that came to hear the "Hallelujah Lasses."

We cannot overlook some of the "characters" the Army uncovered and brought to the Lord. Elijah Cadman could neither read nor write, but he had inscribed on his Bible "Cadman's sword." When he would testify and preach he might hold it upside down. No matter. He had memorized large portions of it. His lack of "book larnin' " only endeared him to the masses and made him a more effective witness.

Then there was "Happy Eliza" Haynes. She was a girl from Booth's home town of Nottingham. With a placard on her back proclaiming, "I am Happy Eliza," and with streamers floating from her jacket and hair she led a spirited gang of young ruffians through the city streets singing one of the army's songs to the tune of "Marching Through Georgia!"

Shout aloud salvation boys! We'll have another song!
Shout it with a spirit that will start the world along
Sing it as our fathers sang it many millions strong,

51

As they went marching to glory!

The burden of human need and unfinished work lay heavy on Booth. "My life," he said, "has been an uninterrupted trial. Often I could weep myself to sleep."

Booth had been working on a book for months. Inspiration for the title came to him one day when he was reading Morton Stanley's best seller *In Darkest Africa*. He would call his book *In Darkest England and The Way Out*. It became a "runaway best seller." It was an expose of the plight of England's poor, but it also contained a plan for alleviating their suffering. It was the contention of Booth that if the state neglects the poor, the public's Christian duty was to step in where the state had failed. He proposed three things: the erection of shelters and industrial homes in the cities, the establishing of farm colonies in the country, and emigration of the poor to more promising parts of the world. The visionary was ahead of his time. He predated American social security by 40 years.

He could hardly have envisioned the storm that was about to break. The book with its revelations and suggested solutions was unpalatable to most. Booth became the most hated and despised of all Englishmen. He was maligned and abused. . .and understandably the most talked about man in England. He had not shunned publicity for himself or the Army in the past. It was good advertising. . .and it was free. But now the banner headlines were about him, and they were barbed and mean.

It is understandable that many might not agree with his philosophy for taking care of the poor, but the vitriolic editorials and opposition of leading men would lead one to suspect that there was a sense of corporate guilt for having done so little for the poor. The conscience of English leadership was smarting because there was someone among them who cared.

But there were better days ahead. Showly the opposition waned. Now not only England was changing but other countries as well. Soon 24 governments were recognizing the work of the Salvation Army and were giving it financial support. The call of the evangelist never left Booth. By now the world had become his parish. By the time he reached his 81st year he had traveled five million miles and preached 60,000 sermons. He loved to preach and the people loved to hear him. Though he was the disciplined authoritarian of the Army in blue, he had his gentler side. He could be humorous and earthy. But his stories strengthened the grip he had on his audience. He often told the story about the young man sobbing at the altar. To Booth's question if he was now converted he blurted out, "I'm a convert allright General, but when I came into this place I'm damned if I had any idea of getting saved."[1]

Booth lived a full life. His wife had preceded him in death by 20 years. It was understandable if the last years had been lonely ones. The white haired and white bearded General had championed a great cause. The price of such an endeavor is always high, but when it touches the family ties, the distress is compounded.

It was probably too much to expect that a man who could mold and discipline such an army could also be a gentle and indulgent father to his children. The problem was that they had been reared in the Army and had risen in the ranks to undershepherds. Had they not been part of the Army it might have been different. But the "General" overshadowed the "Father." One by one, resenting his authoritarian ways, they left to start revival organizations. Only two remained with him. . .his son Bramwell and daughter Evangeline.

The man who had become a legend in his lifetime died August 28, 1912. When once asked what was the secret of his great success, with tears in his eyes Booth responded, "It is because the Lord has had all of me." Perhaps the prostitute said it best, "He cared for the likes of us."

[1]Richard Collier, *The General Next to God*, pp. 362-363.

5

Heinrich Melchoir Muhlenberg (1711-1787)

Lutheran

The special call to God's service did not come with the rendering of the heavens and an audible voice from God. Instead, the "still small voice" was heard at the dinner table amidst good food and Christian fellowship.

It was early fall, September 6, 1741. The headmaster of the University of Halle in Saxony had, as his dinner guest, a young pastor named Heinrich Muhlenberg. As the evening wore on their discussion turned to the subject of Christian missions, a subject that was near to the heart of both men.

Dr. Francke informed his young guest that there had been for some time a desperate cry for help from the German Lutherans in America for pastors, teachers, Bibles, catechisms, prayer books, and printed sermons. But above all was the plea for pastors. He went on to add that since communications by letter had not been productive for the colonists, they had more recently dispatched a delegation of three men to Europe in the hopes of stirring up sympathy for their cause.

In addition to pastors and teachers, they hoped to solicit funds for the building of churches and schoolhouses. Volunteers had presented themselves as candidates for Christian service in the colony, but in the estimate of the Halle leadership it required a particular kind of man. . .one with a rugged constitution, well educated, and with apostolic gifts. Now came the punch line: Would Muhlenberg consider such an assignment, at least for a few years? Would he go to the "Church of the Dispersion" in America? Francke continued to spell out the assignment more specifically, which meant pastoring three congregations in Philadelphia, New Providence, and New Hanover.

Suddenly every fiber of his being was alive. It wasn't a question of would he do it, but rather could he do it? After a few moments of silence, Muhlenberg replied. If this was in the will of God, he would go. He felt bound to go where providence called him.

Young Muhlenberg wasted no time. As soon as he was assured that this was God's call to him, he began to make the necessary preparations. On December 9, "under considerable emotion," he preached his farewell sermon and bade his parishioners goodbye. Eight days later he was aboard ship, bound for England.

Upon arriving in England, he made his way to London. The time spent there was longer than he had expected, but the nine week delay proved to be a blessing in disguise, for during that time he had daily contact with the Lutheran court chaplain, Dr. Ziegenhagen.

Ziegenhagen was an older man, and an important link between the Lutheran leadership of Europe and that of the colonies. This turned out to be the beginning of an enduring relationship between the two. Ziegenhagen was to encourage, guide, and support the young missionary as he took on his important assignment: help alleviate the distress of the Lutheran colonists.

On June 13, 1742, the sailing vessel embarked for America. It was a hazardous undertaking. Besides being unseaworthy, the ship was overloaded, and the prospect of being attacked by pirates was an ever-present danger. As the ship was going out to sea, however, Muhlenberg overheard a poor Salzburg mother singing Luther's "Ein feste Burg" (A Mighty Fortress). He exclaimed, "That is a better protection than the ten cannon with which the vessel is provided."

The voyage to Charleston, South Carolina, was described as one of "unusual peril and exhaustion." The young pastor did not wait until he got to the colonies to begin his missionary labors. The ship became his church, and the passengers, crew, and slaves his mission field. Though he suffered a great deal from seasickness, it did not deter him from taking time to teach and instruct the children, slaves, and others who were interested. On Sunday morning he would preach to the Germans in their own language, and in the afternoon he would have a service for the English speaking people. His English vocabulary was very limited, but that he tried to serve them under such difficult circumstances was, in itself commendable, and for that he was held in high esteem by everyone aboard the ship.

The days on the high seas finally came to an end. It had taken 110 days, but now before them lay Charleston Harbor.

Upon reaching land, Muhlenberg immediately made his way to the German settlement called Ebenezer, some 60 miles from Charleston. This was where the immigrants from Salzburg, Austria, had settled, and Ziegenhagen, was eager that Muhlenberg should make their acquaintance. This he did, but after a brief visit felt compelled to move on.

Fall was setting in and already the vast forestland was a kaleidoscope of brilliant hues. The nights were getting colder and soon winter would be at hand. Between him and his ultimate destination were 900 miles of unbroken wilderness. The question was whether he should proceed by land or by sea. Either way it was a perilous journey, especially this time of year. The fact that he was a stranger to the area and alone only compounded the problem. He chose to go by sea. Though experienced men protested, he set out "in a frail wretched bark, and endured a terrible voyage to Philadelphia."

Upon arriving in Philadelphia on November 25, 1742, he wasted no time in getting in touch with some Germans, and met up with a member of New Hanover Church, which was to be his final destination.

The first Sunday found him in the pulpit of a partially finished log building. The following Sunday he addressed large audiences in Philadelphia, and the third Sunday he conducted services in New Providence. This would be his initial circuit, but as time went on his influence and field of service was to extend along the whole Eastern Sea Board and into the interior.

He was uniquely qualified to bring a scattered remnant under a common banner. The Lutheran Church was like a battered infant, in need of careful nurturing to restore health. This would not be an easy task. The Lutherans had suffered enormous losses to other religious bodies and just plain religious indifference on their part. The gathering, establishing, and uniting of these scattered exiles now would become the life work of Muhlenberg.

Though the first Lutheran church had been established over 100 years before, it had not grown and developed as some of the other church bodies had. It was still fragmented and lacked leadership. Now the necessary leadership had arrived. When Muhlenberg's 45 years of service were over he would have accomplished what no other Lutheran leader had been able to do up to that time, and one historian would say of him, that he was the "outstanding founder of the Lutheran Church in America."

To fully understand how he was able to accomplish what he did, it is necessary to understand something of his spiritual pedigree. He was a son of the Pietistic movement. As a young man of 24 he had entered the University of Gottingen in 1735. He was a man of good moral character and religious upbringing. Knowing that university life was fraught with temptations and pitfalls, he sought out men like himself who were similarly concerned about their spiritual life. He soon found what he was looking for. These men, however, were not cowering in secret behind closed doors. They were on the offensive. They were a part of the spiritual renewal of that day. Muhlenberg joyfully joined their ranks.

Spiritual renewals are seldom wholeheartedly received by the church as a whole. The work of the Spirit often frightens the people and they clothe their fears in concerned opposition. One of the by-products of their attitude is to give the phenomenon a disparaging name. They dubbed the adherents of the renewal "Pietists," because of their love for the Bible, prayer meetings, and witnessing.

A similar movement of the Spirit was sweeping over England. There it was called the "Puritan Revival." Since the fires of the reformation had long hence died down, the Pietistic renewal was God's answer to the hungry hearts crying out for help in that day. It was a "revolt against barren orthodoxy and dead formalism."

The reformation had indeed pointed people to the Bible and had uncovered the basic and fundamental truth that men are justified by faith. But with the passing of years this great and wonderful truth had lost its punch, and the lives of professing Christian people were no different from those in the world. To be sure they were still believers in an intellectual sense, but the citadel of the heart had not been conquered. The Pietists came along and emphasized Christian experienced as a result of genuine repentance and faith toward God.

The Lutheran historian E.J. Wolf points out that Muhlenberg was greatly benefited by his association with men of this caliber. It was through these men that he not only learned of the Pietistic movement, but also learned, among other vital truths, ". . .that the baptism of the Holy Spirit is the indispensible prerequisite for a preacher of the Gospel." The seed-bed that had fed the renewal was the University of Halle in Saxony. Over 6,000 students had gone out from there, spreading the fire of Pentecost to the remote areas of the world. They were a great missionary organization, carrying on missionary work 100 years before what is generally called the beginning of modern missions.

When Muhlenberg began his work in America it took some time before he was accepted by the people. They had been the victims of imposters posing as preachers. Fanatical and disorderly elements had disseminated and now, when a truly worthy man appeared among them, he had to earn his right to be heard.

There was intense opposition at first, but his faithfulness, dignity, personal charm, and the anointing upon his preaching soon won out. Multitudes came to hear him wherever and whenever he came to preach. Believers were fed and the unconverted were awakened. Churches were formally organized, church discipline was introduced, schools were opened, and catechization of the young people was begun. Muhlenberg was in his element here. He loved teaching the youth, and it was not uncommon to have young people, 19 and 20 years old, coming to him "with their ABC books."

His labors took him far afield. He would sometimes ride 30 or 40 miles a day through pathless forests and swollen streams, in the heat of summer and the cold of winter. Rain, snow, and the dark of night were his companions. Many a savage lurking in the bushes watched him go by. Since there were vast distances between settlements, it might be midnight or later before he reached his destination.

When he arrived in a Lutheran community he would go immediately to work. If there was no church building, services would be held under the open sky. There would be the preaching of the Word and the ministering of the sacraments.

Then would follow instructions for the young. If there were problems and divisions, these would be dealt with. Errors would be exposed and undesirable elements would be excluded from the fellowship. He often lamented that lack of time prevented him from caring for the individual sheep as he would have liked. And yet he would go at any hour of night or day to someone needing his help.

In spite of the roads, rivers, and storms, he once said, "One would not like to drag his dog out of the house, yet willingly do I go, at any day or any time left free to me, and visit souls in whom the Spirit has begun His work." It was a common practice for him to spend hours dealing privately with awakened sinners seeking to find peace with God.

Leadership generally had its price, and Muhlenberg was not exempt. He had been no stranger to problems and opposition from without, but that it should rise from within the ranks of his own Lutheran brethren must have grieved him. Because of his ties with the Pietistic movement, his orthodoxy was held in question by men of the Hamburg School who claimed for themselves a "more positive Lutheran orthodoxy."

Muhlenberg was about 65 when the Revolutionary War began. The war brought much carnage and devastation. But the Christian Church survived, as it always does, though badly wounded.

The years had taken their toll on the Lutheran "circuit rider." As Muhlenberg approached 70, he was no longer able to get about as in his youth. But he could look back upon his life with considerable satisfaction. He had ministered the Word to the people on the frontier. He had been present at the birth of a nation, and he had played a central role in unifying and nurturing a fragmented church. His admiring friends did not forget, for on his tombstone was inscribed the following: "Had he no monument, future ages still would know how great a man he was."

6

Brother Lawrence (1605-1691)

Catholic

The night was long and men were feeling their way in the darkness. They cautiously moved forward, hoping they were on the right path. Yet there was much fear and apprehension. What if they were not? Suddenly, a light began to shine. It shone with greater and greater intensity. Like moths attracted to a candle, the pilgrims were drawn to its light. In this case it was a man, one like themselves, and yet he was different. Instead of being bent over by the cares and burdens of life, he seemed to be on vacation, basking in eternal sunshine and refreshing himself from some unseen fountain of youth. Who was he? Why do we still remember him after more than 300 years? It is because the aroma of his life is still with us, and many have learned to sit at his feet and draw upon his wisdom.

Nicholas Herman, better known as Brother Lawrence, was a poor man with little formal education and no theological training. Yet, in the centuries that followed, students, scribes, and theologians have studied his life and pondered the wisdom that he so eagerly and freely shared. It was not that he was profound and complex. . .*that* is our problem. Instead of searching the libraries of the world for wisdom, he had found it at home by himself, in his own circumstance and environment. For it was there he found God. Having thus found the Lord for himself, he maintained that it was simple to know Him and walk with Him. It saddened him to observe the tedious trivia of other men's so-called "devotions" which were so foreign to simple trust in God.

It was here that so many of his fellow workers and others were marooned. They were occupied with trying to rid themselves of sin by penance and good works, instead of looking away from themselves to Jesus Christ who had already dealt with their indebtedness. The needed transformation would come from gazing upon the Savior, not in contemplating their sins. It was the direction of the gaze that made the difference between Brother Lawrence and the men of his order. They were occupied with their sins and what to do with them, and he was occupied with the Savior who had already removed them from the premises. No wonder he spent all of his time, "praising, adoring, and loving Him!"

His conversion seems to have taken place when he was about 18. Often the crisis time of a believer's conversion focuses on a meeting where there are other people, the right kind of climate, and the appropriate means employed to bring the wanderer home. It was not so with Brother Lawrence. What awakened in him a sense of his spiritual need was "the sight in midwinter of a dry and leafless tree and of the reflections it stirred respecting the change the coming spring would bring." From the very beginning he seems to have made a total commitment to God, and sought from that day forward to live continually in His presence. He came to be known as the man who taught "the practice of the presence of God."

Nicholas Herman was a soldier, but in 1666 he applied and was admitted to one of the monastic orders known as the

Carmelites. He became one of the barefoot lay brothers of the order and from that time on was known as Brother Lawrence. He was a big man and gained for himself a reputation as "an awkward fellow who broke everything." One of the reasons for joining this austere order was "that he would then be made too smart for his awkwardness and the faults he should commit, and so he should sacrifice to God his life with its pleasures." But instead of feelings thus dealt with, he had concluded that God instead had "disappointed him. . .having met with nothing but satisfaction in that state."

From what he saw about him, he had reason to question the direction in which his fellow men were moving in their quest for God. There seemed to him to be a great deal of activity that had little value. Spiritual life had become very complex. He concluded in his own mind that there had to be a more simple way. Rules, regulations, self denial, and various other kinds of discipline had their place, but as coins of the kingdom for gaining merit before God, he was not so sure.

He resolved to make another approach, a way that would be more satisfying and fulfilling. He would begin by reckoning for a conscious, personal union between himself and God, and practice it until it became habitual with him. Whether he was aware of it or not at the time he was, in fact, starting out on a sound, Scriptural footing. In the words of another, "The summons of the Gospel is not what we behold what is impossible in Christ and reach for it; but rather that we behold what is accomplished for us in Christ and appropriate it and live in it."[1] To appropriate often requires not only acceptance, but affirmation as well. There is a part of our being that is very unbelieving, and its shouts of resistance and denial can only be overcome and conquered by the hammer blows of affirmation; that is, repeating over and over again some truth of God that you want to experience and realize for yourself.

His practice of the presence of God, though simple, was not so easily attained. It required practice and perseverance. Some may think Brother Lawrence was legalistic and working his way toward God's approval, but this was not true. His emphasis was on faith and love. The results speak for themselves. His view of God, he once said, "kindled in him such love for God that he could not tell whether it had increased during the more-than-40 years that he had lived since." At another time he said his contemplation of God "so inflamed and transported him, that it was difficult for him to contain himself."

The practice of the presence of God, Brother Lawrence maintained, could be done anytime, anywhere. "The times of business," he said, "does not with me differ from the times of prayer; and in the noise and clatter of my kitchen, while several persons are at the same time calling for different things, I possess God in as great tranquility as if I were upon my knees at the blessed sacrament."

His message must have cheered the hearts of many. The common man, because of his daily work schedule, was limited as to how much he could participate in the ongoing program of the church. He was usually able to attend the Sunday services and partake of the sacrament. But unless there was a teaching ministry from the pulpit which acquainted the parishioners with the Word of God, they were like lost sheep. Certainly no amount of religious activity was any substitute for knowing God and His Word — and only that would set them free. Now, however, the encouraging word came from no less than one of their own. God was to be found where they were. It was a matter of faith. God said He had come to live in their hearts. They must believe it and find rest.

It was a wonderful message for the laity. It stood in contrast to the legalistic "churchianity" that was so common in that day. The scrubwoman could worship God as she stroked the washboard. The farmer could look up to God as he lifted that fork full of hay. For the housewife, the kitchen sink became an altar.

It was so simple, and yet it was real. Before, they had brought the fruits of their efforts to God but had walked away empty-hearted. God was asking for hearts and lips that praised Him for what He had done for them, not for something they had done for Him. This they had been doing but were never sure it was enough.

It was the practical side of Christian life that had occupied Brother Lawrence's mind almost from the beginning. Like the modern trouble-shooter, he had set about to find what was wrong with Christian life. It didn't look right, it didn't seem right, and somehow he was convinced it wasn't right. The vitality and reality that the Bible spoke of wasn't there. The abundant life was missing. He might have been tempted to give up, but he didn't. Hannah Whithall Smith wrote, "His one single aim was to bring about a conscious personal union between himself and God, and he took the shortest cut he could find to accomplish it."[2]

That he succeeded in his pursuit we now know. Not only did he find this intimate relationship with God for himself, but he blazed a path clear enough so that others could follow.

It did not come easily. Like most of us, he would stumble and fall, but he persisted. "By rising after my falls," he once said, "and by frequent renewed acts of faith and love, I am come to a state wherein it would be as difficult for me not to think of God as it was at first to accustom myself to do it." No longer was the strenuous effort necessary: "I found myself changed all at once."

His affirmation for a conscious personal union with God had paid off. A great and precious truth had lifted from the pages of the Word of God and had been deposited in his own heart. What he had hungered and thirsted for had become his.

The lessons that Brother Lawrence learned along the way are invaluable to us. When he failed, he did not scold himself or go into depression, for he had learned that he had no resources of his own by which to live a spiritual life. Therefore he had no expectations of himself. When he failed, he would simply acknowledge in words such as, "I shall never do otherwise if You leave me to myself. It is You that must hinder my falling and mend what is amiss." After that he would go on with his work.

Brother Lawrence did not differentiate between the secular and spiritual world. To him they were both alike. To be in prayer in the chapel had no more virtue before God than washing his pots and pans in the kitchen. Every kind of duty was done as unto God. With him, the picking up of a straw, when done under God's direction, was as great a service as any other duty men might otherwise consider great.

It is interesting to note how Brother Lawrence defined his deeper experience with God. He did not use the terms "sanctified," "perfect," "spirit-filled," or employ language such as that of his sister in faith, Madam Guyon, who called it "death to the self-life." I am sure he would have been comfortable with any and all of these terms, had they been a part of his religious vocabulary. Instead he described his state as being "in the bosom of God." He likens himself to the infant at his mother's breast. There were no cares or worries, for his every need was provided for. And as the mother has dreams and expectations for her infant child, so God, too, has great plans for His own child. Only the curtain that separates time from eternity stands in the way of its unfolding.

[1]Source Unknown.
[2]Nicholas Herman of Loraine, *The Practice of the Presence of God*, preface.

7

A.B. Earle
(1812-1895)

Baptist

The ominous winds of unrest and the gathering storm clouds were but precursors of the coming strife. Soon it would be neighbor against neighbor and brother against brother, locked in mortal combat. Scurrying over the land were men carrying guns and bayonets. They were the men of the blue and grey. The Civil War was about to break.

There was another band of men. . .not so many, but they, too, were soldiers. They were soldiers of the cross, and with book in hand, addressed themselves to men and women everywhere. A.B. Earle, a Baptist evangelist, was one of those soldiers.

Earle had begun his ministry about 1830 when he was approximately 18. For the next 50 years he traveled over 200,000 miles through the United States, Canada and England. He preached nearly 20,000 times and saw around 150,000 profess faith in Christ. He was not a sectarian man. His city-wide union campaigns had the support of many denominational churches. He was singularly successful in these efforts. The biographer says that "He deserves to be ranked with the greatest evangelists and soul winners of all time."[1]

Many a sincere observer was mystified because of the success of Earle's ministry. He was not eloquent and had only average powers of delivery. There was nothing about his appearance that would arrest the attention of the listener. He was not emotional, nor did he use the best of language. There was, however, a mysterious power that kept men riveted to their seats while he shared with them the Word of God.

One biographer says, "When he preached on the value of a human soul, I do not remember a single thought or illustration that was new to me; and yet I came away overwhelmed in this realization of the infinite preciousness of each child of Adam, and found myself as I awoke the next morning, weeping in sorrow and anxiety for lost sinners."[2]

There seemed to be a remarkable freedom in Earle's meetings. One of the unique features of his ministry was that it was unpredictable and yet so simple and natural. It was this unexpected direction that a meeting might take which took the unconverted by surprise, before they could erect their defenses.

His preaching was simple and yet pointed. He was a strong believer in the preaching of future punishment, and he was convinced that, "The wicked never flee from the wrath to come until they are fully satisfied that there is wrath." He had one sermon entitled "The sin that hath never forgiveness" (Mark 3:29) which he believed was the means of bringing more than 20,000 to Christ.

Though he was a Christian and an evangelist and had considerable success in his ministry, Earle was not totally satisfied with his own Christian experience. Time and activity had not been able to assuage the discontent that was ever present in the depths of his being. There were times when he would be on the mountain top, but those times would be followed by periods of inner dissatisfaction and depression.

It was the natural outcome of an introspective gaze. Having thus been occupied with looking at himself, he was driven to his knees, confessing his shortcomings and sins. He had yet to learn that this "interior inventory" could only produce distress and that exalted feelings, contentment and fulfillment was the by-product of a mind fixed on the Savior who had come to save mankind from their sins.

Though he had now been in the ministry over 30 years and was past 50, the rest Earle was looking for had eluded him. The story of how he emerged from behind the invisible bars of an unseen prison to the place of victorious living is among the clearest and most Biblical accounts that can be found anywhere. In his book, *Bringing in the Sheaves*, he describes this experience that took him out of the land of instability and brought him to that higher plateau of victorious Christian living.

Earle called it the "Rest of Faith." Through it he learned that his contribution to a satisfying relationship with God is to yield and trust; God will do the rest. Not only did he learn that God would work in his everyday circumstances, but he learned that God had already blessed him "with all spiritual blessing" by virtue of Christ's death on the cross in his behalf.

Ten years earlier a spirit of discontent had begun to gnaw away at his inner being. Earle had an inexpressible hunger to know more of Christ's love, but he did not know how to obtain it. There were times when he had seasons of great joy, and there was the additional satisfaction of seeing many people come to Christ under his ministry. Yet such times were often followed by periods of darkness and doubt.

To compound the problem, believers would come to him for help. They, too, were in distress over their barrenness and lack of joy in their Christian walks. They were spiritually hungry and did not know what to do. But neither could Earle help them. He was an effective soul winner and could lead sinners to peace with God, but he was unable to help believers out of the "slough of despond" and on to the firm ground of rest and contentment.

He did what he could. He shared with them Romans 7, but this was no help. He was only prolonging their day of deliverance by involving them in more do-it-yourself ritual such as more consecrations, more resolutions, and more works.

During such times Earle would be severely tempted. Having little or no resources with which to fend off the darts of the enemy, he would be driven almost to despair. Finally he would look again to the cross. As he gazed again upon the face of Jesus his peace would be restored, and joy would again return, if only for a while.

In the meantime he would ponder such passages as, "If ye abide in me and my words abide in you, ye shall ask what ye will and it shall be done unto you" (John 15:7). He felt certain that there was more being offered than what he had received. Finally the question that loomed large in his life was this: "Can an imperfect Christian sweetly and constantly rest in a perfect Savior, without condemnation?" After pondering this for some time he became satisfied that Christ had made provision for a satisfying Christian experience.

Consequently he procurred a "Consecration book" and on his knees before God he began to write. He committed everything to the Savior and spelled out his resolutions on the pages of the book. He then asked God for grace to carry out his vow. He had supposed that this elaborate and detailed commitment would have ushered him into glory, but in this he was disappointed. From time to time he would renew and repeat his commitment, but to no avail. Because he looked upon his deliverance as something that would take place in the future, he failed to find it for the present.

Now he began to search the inner recesses of his heart for the problem and answer. This only increased his distress for he saw so much that he didn't know was there. Pride, self-will, unbelief, love of the world, and other evil passions, like demons leered at him in his discomfort. It was the "slough of despond" of Pilgrim's Progress. As is so often the case there was one sin that bothered him above all others. . .that of wanting to have his own way when there was disagreement with others.

All along, Earle's intellect had been convinced that victory in Christian life was possible. But how could he get his heart to acquiesce to it? The evidence of the heart's agreement was slow in coming, but as he lived in the facts of the promises and affirmed their reality, his heart began to respond in agreement. With the passing of time temptation seemed to loosen its grip, and it became easier to trust the promises.

He had always enjoyed the ministry of evangelism and yet there was this strange paradox. . .the work was often a great burden to him. Later he learned why. He had been working *for* the Lord instead of *with* Him.

The realization of what his heart had been hungering for evolved gradually, and yet there was a crisis point in which it all blossomed into fullness. "The change," he said, "occurred about 5:00 on November 2, 1863." At first he felt very weak and small, but Jesus became very real to him. Preaching became a great joy and the Lord seemed very near.

Finally he was able to say, "I can sum it all up in a few words and call it, not perfection, not a sinless state, but rest. . .'The Rest of Faith.' " Then he went on to add, "This state of heart is reached only by faith and retained only by faith, not by helping Christ take care of us, but by trusting Him to do it all."

The evangelist continued to preach the same sermons, but now it was different. The load was gone and the results were greater. The sense of God's presence was more noticeable. It was reflected in the solemn faces of the listeners, some of them melting to tears over their sins and others quietly praising God.

His sermon on "Joy of Salvation" in Burlington, Vermont, brought 50 ministers to the altar. The evangelist's argument was this: If a man is filled with the Holy Spirit he has found the key to fullness of joy. This was borne out in his meetings when a man came to the altar seeking the Lord. His wife's religion had never impressed him, but a few days after she had been filled with the Holy Spirit he was so impressed with the change that had come over her that he found no rest until he came seeking the Lord for himself.

Earle was a firm believer in the power of Christian joy. If the pulpit and pew alike could exhibit this divine virtue, he was sure that the man on the street would listen to what they had to say.

[1] James Gilchrist Lawson, *Deeper Experiences of Famous Christians*, p. 301.
[2] Lawson, p. 302.

8

Dwight Lyman Moody (1837-1899)

Interdenominational

The short, stocky man with a full beard and cut-away coat stood on the platform of the mammoth hall in Kansas City. It was Thursday night, only the fifth evening into the series of special services, but the weakened heart of the evangelist could no longer continue. This would be his last service. Before him was a sea of friendly and sympathetic faces who hung on his every word. He had finished his message, given the invitation, and closed the meeting. The pose he now struck was a familiar one. Leaning out over the platform with an outstretched arm he pronounced his usual benediction, but this time it was to be his last: "Goodnight, and I'll see you in the morning." Thus ended the evangelistic ministry of the "Commoner of Northfield," D.L. Moody.

D.L., as he was commonly known, was born in Northfield, Massachusetts, February 5, 1837. He was the sixth child in a family of nine. The family was of Puritan stock and he could trace his ancestry back seven generations. For 200 years his forebears had lived and worked their farms in the Connecticut Valley.

His father died at the age of 41. Extreme poverty overtook the family and they lost everything. Through the help of a couple of uncles they were partially provided for, and his mother was able to keep her brood together. The family remained poor, but his mother did her best to bring her children up as a Christian mother should.

Moody left the farm when he was 17. He had an uncle in Boston, so he headed for the bright lights to seek out his fortune.

He did very well as a shoe salesman in his uncle's store. On Sunday he could be found at the Mt. Vernon Congregational Church, where he became an active member of the Sunday School. His teacher, Mr. Kimball, took special interest in him, and one day approached him at his work about personally committing himself to Christ. Moody was ready, and there in the back room of the store he gave his heart to God. Now he had a testimony. It was very simple. . .and it was very good. "Before my conversion," he said, "I worked *toward* the cross, but since then I have worked *from* the cross; then I worked to *be* saved, now I *am* saved."[1]

Working with his uncle became a bit confining for this young dynamo, and he longed for greener pastures. The stirrings were already in his heart. He would head for that flourishing metropolis of the West. . .Chicago.

The spring of 1858 found him in the shoe business again, but this time as a commercial traveler for C.N. Henderson. By "steamboat, rig, horseback and train" he traversed a half dozen of the Midwestern states, but he was usually back in Chicago on the weekend.

Sunday School was his first love. Though, as a lad of 17 in Boston, he was once unable to find the Gospel of John, he now gathered the urchins off the streets and began to instruct them. When the class got too big, he divided it. Putting others in charge, out he went again to find some more.

After a while he built his own Sunday School and church. In time he had over a thousand children enrolled in classes. Because of his way with children and his mode of operation, some called him "Crazy Moody." But his promotional methods were effective. Soon his Sunday School was the envy of other churches, for it outstripped them all in attendance.

Moody had little formal education and no Bible training, but he had the ability to express himself as well as a vision and a passion for souls. In time he began to preach. Haltingly at first, he would usually take a Scripture text and use it as a starter for his own train of thought. That his sermons were deficient in Scripture content had not occurred to him. But eager to learn, he set about to meet and hear the leading scholars and preachers of his day.

This led him to embark for England. He wanted to meet and hear the great English preacher, C.H. Spurgeon, a man approximately his own age. He had read everything he possibly could that Spurgeon had written. Coming to England he soon found himself in the third balcony of the beautiful tabernacle, weeping as he listened to the young minister unfold the Word of God. The horizon grew larger as he envisioned what God would do in Chicago.

While still in England, something happened that was destined to be one of the critical junctures in the road for Moody and his future ministry.

A young man by the name of Moorehouse approached him one day, after he had preached, and said words to the effect that, "If you will begin to preach what God says instead of what you *think* He says, He will make a great preacher out of you."

What Moody's response was isn't known, but the young man had taken a liking to Moody, and wanted to return to Chicago with him. Moody gave him the slip and left without him, only to be followed in a few weeks by the young Englishman. He headed straight for Moody's home. Moody was amazed to hear this young man as he expounded for one whole week on John 3:16. Moody later said, "I never knew up to that time that God loved us so much." The result was that, realizing he would have to know his Bible better, he rose at 6:00 every morning for the rest of his life to study the Word of God. He became an excellent expositor of the Word.

Moody had long since stopped selling shoes, and now gave all his time to Christian work. He was one of the leading young lights of the Y.M.C.A. But with all his activity and seeming success, his heart grew restless. Adding to his frustration was the fact that there were a couple of Free Methodist ladies in his congregation who said they were praying for him. This was fine, but when they kept reminding him of this, he replied, "Why don't you pray for the people?" They believed he needed more power was their answer. After several months he swallowed his pride and came to them for counsel. What did they mean by "more power"?

These daughters of Methodism "expounded to him the way of God more perfectly," not for salvation, but for the baptism of the Holy Spirit. This was followed by prayer for this enduing of power.

It was some time before the truth of this transaction was realized. Moody seldom spoke of it. It was such a personal matter. R.A. Torrey gives us a glimpse into what happened. Moody was walking up Wall Street when he became overwhelmed with the near presence of God. He stopped at a friend's house and asked if he might have a room where he could be alone for a while. This was gladly granted. He remained there for hours. The Holy Spirit filled him with such joy and power that at last he had to ask God to "withhold His hand lest he die."

The doctrine of the baptism of the Holy Spirit then, as now, was not always so palatable in some circles. This disturbed Moody greatly. He had teachers in his own schools who did not believe in a personal baptism. One day he called on Torrey to come to his home and talk to his teachers.

Moody and Torrey talked to the teachers for some time, but were unable to persuade them of the need for this personal baptism. As the students were leaving Moody signalled Torrey to remain for a few minutes. Moody was distressed. "Oh, why will they split hairs?" He acknowledged that they were good teachers, but he believed that the baptism of the Holy Ghost was the one touch that they needed.

After his anointing for service, Moody was a different man. He preached the same sermons but the results were much greater. More and more people came to Christ.

He returned to England. Ira D. Sankey would play his portable organ and sing, "Dare To Be A Daniel" and "The Ninety And Nine." Moody would preach and gather in the sinners. Sankey set two continents to singing and Moody set them to thinking about God.

They held services in England, Scotland, and Ireland, and after two years, when they were getting ready to return to their homeland, there was not a building large enough to accommodate the crowds.

After Moody's return home there loomed ahead of him yet another great challenge. It was a mammoth undertaking, a project on such a scale as had never been tried before. It would be a well planned and coordinated Gospel thrust into the upcoming world's fair of 1893. Moody, with the help of businessmen, preachers, and gospel workers, undertook the project. People were not accustomed to attending the circus under the "big top" on Sunday, so gospel services were held there instead. Ten thousand people would pack the big tent on a hot summer day to hear the voice of this illustrious but humble servant of God.

Then came the San Francisco crusade in the Cow Palace. The evening service was about to begin. As Moody was leaving his hotel room, someone handed him his mail, which included a letter edged in black from England. Hurriedly he tore open the letter. Moorehouse, the young Englishman, was dead at the age of 39. Overcome with emotion, he returned to his room. As the tears flowed, he gazed out the window and saw the masses of people moving through the streets and avenues to the Cow Palace for the evening service. Again he remembered the prophetic words of this young man, "If you will begin to preach what God says instead of what you think He says, He will make a great preacher out of you."

The years rolled by and Moody's heart began to fail him. In the final hours on his deathbed, he moved in and out of a coma. At one point he said to his wife, "If this is death there is no valley. This is glorious. I have been within the gates, and I saw the children! (referring to two deceased grandchildren of whom he had been very fond). Earth is receding; heaven is approaching! God is calling me!"[2]

[1]Richard Ellsworth Day, *Bush Aglow*, p. 72.
[2]Day, p. 330.

9

Smith Wigglesworth (1859-1946)

Pentecostal

The plumber was near death. For the past six months his appendix had troubled him. Now his condition was so serious and his body so weak that an operation was out of the question. The doctor could do nothing, but promised to look in on his patient later in the day.

It was a sad and desperate hour for the young wife who would be left with small children to care for and no means of support. But just as the doctor was leaving, a woman and her young son arrived. She was no ordinary woman. She had not come to sympathize with the family nor had she come to comfort the sick and dying. Taking command of the situation, she proceeded to plead the man's case before the bar of God. As she stormed the gates of heaven, she reminded her heavenly Father of His promises and of how He had come to her assistance in times past.

The son, too, was equally well schooled in the art of authority. When his mother began to pray he positioned himself atop the weakened body and began jabbing his fists into the man's stomach. It was an incredible sight. As he pummeled the man's body he kept shouting, "Come out, devil, in the name of Jesus."

When the session was over, the man rose from his bed completely well. Going downstairs to his plumbing shop he proceeded to take care of a work order that had come in.

When the doctor returned the man's wife cried triumphantly that her husband had gone out on an errand. Shocked, he replied, "They will bring him back as a corpse as sure as you live." But the "corpse" lived to be 87 years of age and left a legacy to mankind quite unequaled in his time.

Smith Wigglesworth was born in 1859 in a humble shack in Menston, in Yorkshire, England. It was the year of the great revival. What had begun as a religious awakening in the United States in 1857 had now reached the shores of the British Isles. It was a welcome diversion from the drudgery of everyday life. If hard labor kept them in bondage, at least many were now free in their hearts and could sing the songs of Zion.

Wigglesworth was only six years old when he began to work in the fields, pulling and cleaning turnips. At night his hands would be sore and bleeding. When he was seven he began to work in the woolen mill where his father was a weaver. The hours were long. He would rise at 5:00 in the morning, grab a bite to eat, walk the two miles and report for work at 6:00. "We had to work 12 hours a day," he said, "and I often said to my father, 'It's a long time from six until six in the mill.' I can remember the tears in his eyes as he said, 'Well, 6:00 will always come.'"

The little boy had always had a longing for God. Though his parents were not professing Christians, he did have a godly grandmother. She belonged to the Wesleyan Methodist church and often took her young grandson to the meetings. As an eight-year-old he remembered how the good Methodist folk would gather at 7:00 on Sunday morning. They would dance around the big stove in the center of the church and clap their hands and sing:

"Oh, the Lamb, the bleeding Lamb,
The Lamb of Calvary,
The Lamb that was slain,
To intercede for me."

He later said, "As I clapped my hands and sang with them, a clear knowledge of the new birth came into my soul. I looked to the Lamb of Calvary. I believed that He loved me and had died for me. Life came in—eternal life—and I knew that I had received a new life which had come from God."

Thus it was that an eight-year-old boy, ready to go to work in the kingdom, tenderly approached his mother and led her to Christ.

Wigglesworth's father encouraged his children to attend the Episcopal Church. It was not that he was a churchgoer, but he was a good friend of the parson, a congenial fellow. They often drank together at the local pub.

For the children, this checkered religious upbringing could have been a liability. To be shunted from one religious tradition to another does not usually lend itself to Christian stability, but it did give young Wigglesworth a religious overview and tolerance for others he might not otherwise have had. Years later he commented on his religious upbringing. He had come to Christ under the ministry of the Methodists. Then he was confirmed by the Bishop in the Church of England. He was later immersed as a Baptist. He became indebted to the Plymouth Brethren for his grounding in the Bible, and, finally, he became one of the foremost of leaders among the classical Pentecostals. Although he never joined a religious body, he belongs among the early lights in the Pentecostal movement.

At the age of 18 he began his apprenticeship as a plumber. He was a good worker and learned the trade rapidly. By the time he was 20 he had moved to Liverpool. Here he continued to ply his trade, but he would spend all his evenings helping the poor. His heart especially went out to the young people, many of them orphaned and living on the streets. Wigglesworth would gather them together in some shed or on the docks, provide them with food and then lead them to Christ.

Active as he was in Christian work, he had great difficulty expressing himself. When called upon to speak in some Salvation Army meeting he invariably broke down and began to weep. Instead of disturbing the meeting, this only endeared him to the listeners.

By the time he was 23 he had opened his own plumbing business. He continued to work with the Salvation Army as time would allow. These were rewarding days as he saw men and women changed by the power of God.

One evening the speaker at a Salvation Army outdoor service was Tillie Smith, sister of the well-known evangelist Gypsy Smith. She brought a powerful message and when the invitation was given a young lady named Mary Jane Featherstone was among the first to respond and come forward. Kneeling at the altar rail the evangelist led her to Christ. When assurance came to her heart she jumped to her feet, threw her gloves in the air and with typical Methodist enthusiasm shouted, "Hallelujah, it is done."

Smith Wigglesworth was in the audience that night and was more than just a casual observer. The young lady had caught his attention. At the close of the service he made haste to make her acquaintance—a romance was in the making.

Mary Jane, or Polly as she came to be known, made rapid progress in her Christian life. Her association with the Gypsy evangelists soon brought her in contact with the leading figure of the Salvation Army, the General himself, William Booth. He was sufficiently impressed with Polly and her Christian progress so that he offered her an officer's commission without the usual boot training. She graciously accepted the honor, but later discovered that fraternizing between officers and soldiers was forbidden. Reluctantly, she resigned her commission and followed her heart. It led straight to the altar where she and Wigglesworth were married.

At 22 Polly was already an outstanding soul winner. Her husband, now 23, had already established himself as an able worker among the needy. In order to fulfill the divine assignment which was yet to unfold, he needed a co-worker of Polly's caliber. He himself once said, "She saw how ignorant I was and immediately began to teach me to read properly and write; unfortunately, she never succeeded in teaching me to spell."

In the service it was Polly who did the preaching. She was young, vivacious, and eloquent. While she was exhorting the people, Wigglesworth would care for the children. But when it was time for personal work at the altar rail, he would be ready and waiting. This was his forte.

Wigglesworth continued in the plumbing business, but the demand upon his time caused him to neglect his spiritual life until his backslidden condition was evident to all, especially his wife. The estrangement took on a humorous vein one evening when she returned later than usual from the evening service. As she walked in the door her husband remarked, "I am the master of this house, and I am not going to have you coming home so late an hour as this." His wife quietly replied, "I know that you are my husband, but Christ is my Master." This angered him and he firmly escorted her out the back door, but he had forgotten to lock the front door. In a matter of moments she was back in the house, laughing. She laughed so heartily that he, too, began to laugh, and thus the "incident" was resolved.

Polly's patience with her husband paid off, and soon they were of one heart and mind in their labors.

Wigglesworth would periodically go to Leeds for his plumbing supplies. While there he learned of a healing service being held. His curiosity led him to investigate and he came home impressed as he saw people healed before his eyes. At first he did not tell Polly, for he was sure she would consider it fanaticism. When she finally did learn of the meetings and of her husband's interest, she, too, became interested, perhaps because of her own personal need. On the next business trip to Leeds, Polly accompanied her husband. They attended the healing meetings, and she received what she had secretly come for—her own personal healing.

Wigglesworth, as has been pointed out, was unusually gifted as a personal worker. His wisdom and patience in dealing with needy men resulted in someone being touched for God almost every day. His relationship with God could not be hidden. "Tell me, oh, please tell me," said a woman, "what is the cause of your face showing such a wonderful expression of joy?" To which he replied, "Well, this morning two of my children came to the breakfast table very sick. My wife and I prayed for them and God instantly healed them. I was filled with joy as I saw what He had wrought, and that joy is with me now." His answer to the lady only stirred her heart the more and she replied, "Please tell me how to get this joy. My house is full of trouble." As she continued to ruminate about her problem-filled life, God's messenger gently guided the hungry soul into the green pastures of God's provision and she, too, became the possessor of this peace and joy.

In the early days of the Pentecostal movement, much tension centered around the gifts of tongues and healing. Many who were involved in the awakening believed there were two kinds of tongues, the one which the evidence that the individual had been baptized with the Holy Spirit, and the other which was exercised in the private devotional life or in the public assembly if an interpreter was present. Curiosity drove some of the bystanders to investigate this phenomenon, Wigglesworth among them.

He was especially intrigued by the gift of tongues and the manifestations of healing that he saw. Though he had experienced sanctification as the Methodists taught it, he now concluded that the baptism with the Spirit, followed by the evidence of speaking in tongues, was the true Pentecostal baptism. This he sought and received.

After this new encounter with God, Wigglesworth returned home, only to find that his wife was very suspicious about the "new wine" he had been imbibing. In a defensive mood she said, "I want you to understand that I am as much baptized as you are, and I don't speak in tongues. I have been preaching for 20 years," she continued, "and you have sat beside me on the platform, but on Sunday you will preach yourself, and I'll see what there is in it."

They had been a team; now the tables had turned. He was beginning to assert himself, and under the anointing of God his shyness and reticence vanished.

Stepping to the podium, the following evening, he read his text. It was from Isaiah 61:1-3.

It was like opening a barrage of gunfire on his audience. The people were amazed and stunned to hear the authority with which he spoke. His wife, sitting in the back of the hall, was greatly agitated. Unable to stand it any longer, she blurted out so all could hear, "That's not my Smith, Lord, that's not my Smith."

But as the evening service progressed, she was convinced. Soon she, too, sought and found what her husband was talking about, and unity and harmony was again restored in the Wigglesworth household. In reminiscing about those days he added that, as a result of those meetings, "Hundreds had received the baptism in the Holy Ghost and all of them spoke in tongues."

Calls began to come in for his services. Together he and his wife launched out with renewed enthusiasm. People were saved, healed, and baptized with the Holy Spirit. Hundreds and sometimes thousands flocked to hear them as they shared the reality of God with their listeners.

It was not always easy. Opposition rose from almost every

quarter. His activity stirred and disturbed the demonic world. He was to learn that demons not only plague mankind, but at times were found embedded in human personalities. With time he learned to detect them and expel them in the name of Jesus.

In time, the ministry at home reached to the neighboring communities. Then the beckoning call could be heard from afar. The Wigglesworths travelled to Switzerland, Scandinavia, the United States, Australia, New Zealand, India, Ceylon, and South Africa.

Wigglesworth tells of his ministry in Columbo where the weather was hot and stifling, sometimes 120°. The place was packed with many sick people, and sometimes 50 or more with babies in their arms. When he began he would say, "Before I preach I will minister to the babies." He would then pray and lay his hands on each of them, and soon all was quiet and peaceful.

This miraculous calm did not go unnoticed and it engendered expectant faith for the remaining part of the service. Healings would take place before he was through speaking. One evening a man, who had been blind for years, was instantly healed. Such was the level of faith so that miracles constantly followed this ministry.

When he went to New Zealand he had just one man who met him when he disembarked from the ship. After a few months, however, it was acknowledged that the revival that followed in his footsteps was the greatest spiritual awakening in that land in a century.

Wigglesworth's ministry in the Scandinavian lands was equally exciting and gratifying. There was no place large enough to accommodate the multitudes. The pattern was always the same. Under his ministry the people were saved, healed, and baptized with the Spirit. But as the ministry became known and its influence felt, opposition would invariably follow.

Wigglesworth had served with joy in the vineyard of the Lord, but it had not been without cost. His wife and co-worker was only 53 when she was called home in 1913.

The last decade of his life was one of continual ministry to others. But strangely, the man who had been so mightily used to carry the gifts of healing to others, was himself in failing health. The doctor urged him to submit to an operation, but his reply was, "Doctor, the Lord who made this body is the one who can cure it. No knife shall ever cut it so long as I live." Consequently, there were years of intense suffering. Yet his faith stood firm as he ministered to the needs of others until the time of his death at age 87.

10

George Muller
(1805-1898)

Plymouth Brethren

The tall, lean man, then in his 92nd year, was busy at his desk compiling and recording figures. The periodic report was a practice of long standing. But this one would be different. It would also be his last. Statistics alone could not tell the story, so woven into the tapestry of the document was the story of this man's ministry. It would be a treatise in honor of a Father who had so graciously led and provided for his offspring.

It was 63 years earlier that the Father had taken his son into partnership with Himself and had given him a verse from Psalm 81:10, "Open thy mouth wide and I will fill it."

From that day the young man did not deviate from his divinely appointed goal. . .to ask and receive so that a world might know that there is a God in heaven who can be trusted, and who hears and answers prayer.

George Muller was the son of a government revenue collector. He was born in Prussia (now East Germany) in 1805. He had ample reason to be grateful for the way God had blessed him.

Muller had gotten a wrong start in life. An indulgent father had allowed his two sons too much leisure time and too much money. The result was that this ten-year-old boy was well on his way to ruination. Though his weekly allowance was more than he should have had it was not enough for young George, so he began to steal from the government coffers of which his father was in charge. It would have been difficult for anyone who knew him in those early days to have envisioned the great man he was destined to become.

By his own admission his wicked lifestyle was described as one of "lying, stealing, gambling. . .licentiousness, extravagance and almost every form of sin."

At the age of 10 he was sent away to school that he might begin preparation for the Christian ministry. His father was most anxious that his son become a Lutheran minister in the state church, in order that he might have "an easy and comfortable living."

When he was 14 he was confirmed. A part of the confirmation exercise was the taking of his first communion. It should have been a memorable occasion and yet it was not. That he had been involved in "gross immorality" just a few days prior to this sacred event seems not to have troubled him at all.

The proddings of conscience, if any, were at first too gentle to effect any outward change, but as the penalties of wrongdoing began to catch up with him he had opportunity to reflect on his wayward course and where it could possibly end.

Such an opportunity came when he was thrown into jail for attempting to defraud an innkeeper of his rent which was due. It was a sobering experience for a boy of only 16. It was also an angry father who met him on his return home. But the thrashing he got, far from reforming him, only alerted him to the need of being more subtle in his devious ways. So, for the time being, he set about to mend the rift now existing between himself and others. His outward conduct became exemplary and slowly he wormed his way back into the good graces of all around him.

His next few years were spent in school where he became proficient in Latin, French, and the history of his own German language. He was a good student and held in high esteem by his fellows and teachers, but he later acknowledged that he did not care in the least about God. Yet there were times when more serious thoughts would engage his mind. These would be followed by resolutions to reform, only to fail under the pressure of the next temptation.

When he was 20 he entered the Divinity School at the University of Halle. This grand old institution, in an earlier day, had been the spiritual center of Europe. Out from its classrooms had gone more than 6,000 spirit-filled men and women who had traversed the globe doing God's work. But now the fire had gone out. Humanism and rationalism had dealt it a death blow. Only a few smoking embers remained. Muller, in reflecting on those earlier days at the university, believed that only about nine students out of the 900 were really born again.

As a divinity student he was now eligible to preach in the Lutheran State Church. But George Muller had not changed. He was still the conniving, cheating, lying rogue he had always been. If anything he seemed to be even worse than before. But his outward behavior belied the hungry, seeking heart within.

The only way he knew how to respond to the pangs of conviction was to drown himself in the pleasures available. One such example was an excursion that took place during a school vacation. With forged passports, he and a group of his friends embarked for Switzerland. Again, in his financial need, he resorted to cheating his friends, and later lying to his father about his trip.

It was an obscure and unexpected event that terminated the

wicked part of Muller's life. His friend, Beta, invited him to a Saturday night home meeting. Muller was impressed with the gracious welcome they received. For a religious meeting, it was different than anything he had ever known before. There was no clergyman present so they were limited by law as to what they could do. There could be no preaching or teaching, but they could sing, pray, read the Scriptures, and read a written sermon—which they did. The beautiful climate of Christian fellowship was also new to Muller, but what he would never forget was how they would kneel and pray at the opening and the close of the service. Muller had been so absorbed in what he saw, what he heard and what they did that he had not noticed how his own feelings had been elevated to an extremely happy state.

As they were walking home he shared this with Beta, and went on to add that all the former pleasures he had ever known did not begin to compare with what he had experienced that evening. He often said later that he believed that was the time God had chosen to begin a work of grace in his heart.

Though there was not any deep sorrow and scarcely any knowledge, his life's direction had been completely reversed. He could not wait until the next Saturday night meeting, but returned to the house two or three times during the week that he might read the Scriptures and have prayer with his new found friends.

Muller's encounter with God produced a revolutionary lifestyle. He parted company with his wicked friends, gave up going to the tavern, and his notorious habit of lying was terminated. Instead he gave himself to the study of the Scriptures, prayer, church attendance, and the fellowship of like-minded believers.

Though he was now a happy man and making rapid progress in his Christian life, it was not without heartaches. In his enthusiasm he had written to his father and brother about his conversion to Christ. He had gone on to encourage them to make similar commitments. The hoped-for letter of good news did not come. Instead an angry missive was the response. They had become incensed. The father, especially, was greatly disappointed that his son was turning his back on the Lutheran ministry and the state church to become a missionary. He felt that all the effort to educate his son had been for naught.

The early period in the life of a new believer is a time of adjustment and growth. It is not altogether strange if he finds himself confused. So it was with Muller. His friends at the university were laughing at him and his own loved ones had rejected him. There was a momentary solace when he struck up a relationship with a young lady, but this so drew his mind away from Christ that he was left in a deeper state of confusion.

One day, however, a precious scene evolved before his eyes. He had observed a young missionary candidate giving up all his luxuries and his beautiful home that he might serve Christ. In that instant his eyes were opened to see how far he was off course and how selfish he had been.

During Muller's stay at the university the little group of believers grew from six to 20. They would meet in each other's rooms and would spend the time singing, reading the Bible, and praying.

He was 22 when he volunteered to go as a missionary to the Germans in Bucharest, but war between the Turks and the Russians prevented this. Later he offered his services to the London Missionary Society to go as a missionary to the Jews. He was well versed in the Hebrew language and felt that he could be of help to them. But the society wanted to meet him in person first, so he was asked to come to London. It was not the robust missionary candidate who reported to the society, but a frail and weak man who was further handicapped in that he was among a people whose language he could neither understand nor speak.

Illness continued to plague him such that he believed he was going to die. Yet he was not distressed. "I longed exceedingly to depart and be with Christ,'' he said. It was a disappointed man who heard the doctors pronounce that he was getting better.

Muller did not have to look beyond England for his mission field, however. Whether he knew it or not, he had already arrived. A German missionary in England? Yes. Before he could launch out to fulfill his life's calling, however, there was yet a further work for God to do in him. His illness had helped prepare the way. It had brought him to a place of total commitment to God. ''I gave myself fully to the Lord,'' he said, ''Honor, pleasures, money, my physical powers, all were laid at the feet of Jesus, and I became a lover of the Word of God.''

Because of his ill health he had been advised to spend some time in the country. It was here in company with a spirit-filled pastor that his eyes were opened to see that the Holy Spirit could give life to the Scriptures and be the teacher of his people. He was greatly blessed as he heard this man preach. He was further encouraged and enlightened as they fellowshipped together in the Word and in prayer.

Muller had never understood the office and function of the Holy Spirit before this time. Now, however, in just one evening spent in reading the Scriptures, meditation and prayer he said he learned more than he had learned over a period of several months previously.

When he returned to the seminary he was anxious to lead his friends into a deeper walk with God. He was not disappointed. God had prepared candidates and they were open to what Muller had to share. The result was they began to give themselves to prayer—prayer that would last till midnight and later. A few times it was 2:00 a.m. before they dispersed, and even then Muller said they were so full of joy they could hardly sleep and by 6:00 they came together again for prayer.

The well-known Boston preacher, A.J. Gordon, was granted a brief interview with Muller. He wanted to know more about his Christian experience. Muller told of his conversion, but added that the years following had been barren years. Then he mentioned how he and a few of his friends began to seek God for the "gift of the Spirit." "He came to us with such power that at times it was impossible for me to leave Him. His power was so sweet and so entrancing; and I knew what it meant to be baptized with the Holy Ghost," Muller said.

Muller became pastor of an independent church called Ebenezer Chapel in Teignmouth, Devonshire. It was here that he met Mary Groves who was later to become his wife.

He was an innovator from the beginning. Instead of accepting the regular pastor's salary he chose rather to live by faith, telling no one of his needs but God. The system of pew rental was not to his liking either. He felt that it catered to the better classes and the wealthy at the expense of the poor. The practice was abandoned.

His stay at Ebenezer was brief. Soon he was called to serve as pastor of Bethesda Church in Bristol. (This church was affiliated with the Plymouth Brethren.) Within 10 days of his coming the crowds were so large it took four hours to minister to them. He served that church for the remaining days of his life, about 62 years, and when he died the church had a communicant membership of about 2,000.

He was 29 when he founded the Scripture Knowledge Institution. Its purpose was to assist day schools, missionaries, and to circulate the Scriptures and other religious books.

It was Muller's work among orphans, however, that made him a household name throughout the world. Starting with a rented building and a few orphans, the project began to grow. Soon he was adding other buildings to accommodate additional orphans.

The time came when he felt the Lord wanted him to begin erecting his own buildings. In time five huge and beautiful homes graced the grounds. It was a monument to God's greatness, for it had all materialized in answer to prayer. A man who at first could only trust God for very small sums, in due time was able to trust Him for buildings, their upkeep, and the needs and provisions of as many as 2,000 orphans, as well as maintaining the Institution.

The testings had been, at times, severe. Nevertheless, the children were always provided for. There was never a time when they went without a meal.

At an age when most men have retired, Muller launched out into yet another facet of ministry. He was 70 when he began to travel abroad. He made 17 trips, traveling 200,000 miles. It is estimated that during this time he addressed about three million people. The lessons of faith he had learned with his orphans in Bristol he was eager to share with others.

His faith, too, was very active. He lived this life day by day. On one occasion, when crossing the Atlantic, the fog was so dense that the ship captain had to reduce the speed of the ship and travel gingerly among the icebergs of the North Atlantic. The captain, having relayed this information to Muller, was surprised when his guest remarked that he had an appointment in Canada at a certain time and date and he expected to be there on time. But at the speed the ship was now traveling there was no way they could reach the Canadian shore in time.

Muller, not at all disturbed, suggested that they go down to the captain's room and pray about the matter. This they did. Muller began to pray. The captain was intrigued; Muller addressed God as someone whom he knew well. There was no ranting and raving and storming the gates of heaven, but a simple request and then an expression of thanks that the request had been honored. Having ended his prayer, the captain felt obliged to also pray. But as he began, Muller rose from his kneeling position and tapped the captain on the shoulder. He simply said that no further prayer was necessary. He reminded the captain that he did not really believe, and furthermore the fog had already lifted. Going topside again they found the fog had indeed dispersed and the sun was shining brightly.

The apostle of faith lived to be 93. It is estimated that he had trusted God for more than $7,000,000. The young lad who started out so badly as a youth was redeemed by the grace of God and lived to share the goodness of God with millions.

11

Oswald Chambers (1874-1917)

Baptist

The service was over. A father, with his little boy trudging beside him, was on his way home. It was the little lad who broke the silence by volunteering that, if an invitation had been given, he would have responded and given his heart to God. The father, who was also himself a pastor, replied, "You can do it now, my boy." Then and there, in the street, father and son brought the little boy's petition before God. The gospel invitation was accepted, and the transaction was consummated. The little boy, in his own way, had validated the earlier commitment of father and mother on his behalf.

Oswald Chambers was destined for a unique life and ministry. His unconventional ways and the absence of religiosity, coupled with a brilliant and sanctified intellect, gave him an open door to the hearts of needy men. He seems to have had premonitions of his high calling. "From my very childhood," he once said, "the persuasion has been that of a work strange and great, an experience deep and peculiar.

It has haunted me ever and ever." Another time he said, "I feel I shall be buried for a time, hidden away in obscurity; then suddenly, I shall flame out and be gone." How prophetic were these words. He was only 43 when the final summons came. His departure seemed to many an insurmountable loss. Yet today he speaks more eloquently and to many more people, for he wrote over 30 books. The theme running through all of these volumes could well be summarized in the title of one of the earliest and best known of his books, *My Utmost For His Highest*.

In case the reader might think that Oswald Chambers had "easy passage" to the heights of God, let him note what Chambers once said: "Do I need to refer to the night when I speak of the sunrise? Do I need to tell you of the blazing fiery furnace when I speak of the pure gold? Do I need to tell of the quarry blast or the mallet and chisel when I speak of the statue?"

Chambers had expected that his life's work would be in the field of art. Consequently, he trained at the art school in South Kensington where he obtained a master's degree in art. Later he returned to Scotland where he took the arts course at Edinburgh University. He was an excellent student, and was considered by many a master craftsman in his field. While at South Kensington he won a scholarship for two years of travel to the famous art centers abroad. But as he observed the lifestyle of this class of people he became apprehensive. Many had returned from these tours abroad both moral and physical wrecks.

It was while still at Edinburgh that the unmistakable call of God came to him. Like an audible voice he seemed to hear, "I want you in My service—but I can do without you." He did not hesitate to obey. "I recall," he said, "the turmoil when the strongly realized, but yet little understood, call for His work came, and I ruthlessly arrested my life and wrenched it round and hurt and hit badly."

After his decision to serve the Lord, Chambers felt led to apply for entrance to a small Bible college known as Dunoon. The founding father of this modest effort was the Reverend Duncan McGregor. He began by gathering young Christian men around him and teaching them theology, Hebrew and Greek.

With the arrival of Oswald Chambers, now 23, the school leadership recognized it had a young man in its midst of more than average talent, vision, and Christian commitment. His rapid progress enabled him the following year to help in carrying a part of the teaching load. In addition to his own studies, he now began to teach classes in logic, moral philosophy, and psychology. He was now in his element. He always looked upon his years at Dunoon as the most important preparatory years of his life.

These were difficult years for the young man. The conscious relationship with God that he had enjoyed from his youth was missing. It was the "dark night of the soul" for this trainee. Here was a man who was gifted, sincere, and consecrated, but that was not enough. If he were to do battle in the arena in which the souls of men are at stake, he would have to be further trained and tested.

This time of testing was not long in coming. There was slander and misunderstanding of all kinds. Chambers was avoided and evil was spoken of him. As if that were not enough, when a request came for a student speaker from the college, those Scotsmen were careful to spell out who they did not want. "Dinna send us yon long haired swearing parson." He was to say in later years, "Immediately, when you are prepared to live in the inspiration of your ideals, you will become a speckled bird."

Chambers had from his earliest years enjoyed the presence of God in his life and he was always ready for steps of obedience that would draw him nearer to the Savior. It was while he was a tutor of philosophy at Dunoon College that a new challenge confronted him. The well-known Dr. F.B. Meyer had come there to speak to the students on the Holy Spirit. Chambers was impressed with what he heard and after the service he went home, got down on his knees and asked God for the baptism of the Holy Spirit, "whatever that meant."

But instead of life getting better it got worse. The Spirit of God began to deal with him. He began to show Chambers what he was like. When he saw the depravity of his nature, he all but despaired. Later he was to say that the following four years were so awful that, "Nothing, but the overruling grace of God and the kindness of friends kept him out of an asylum." During those years there were very few that understood him, nor did he understand himself. He didn't know anyone that had what he wanted. In fact, he did not know what he wanted. There was no conscious communion with God, the Bible was the dullest of books, and in his own mind he had come to the conclusion that if what he had was all there was to Christianity it was a fraud.

As he pondered his dilemma he began to consider Luke 11:13, "If ye then being evil know how to give good gifts to your children, how much more shall your heavenly Father give the Holy Spirit to them that ask him." Certainly Chambers would qualify as a recipient for he knew he was evil—just as the text said. But he was also considered by the school and others as a "prize catch." This was why he was elevated to carry a part-time teaching load while still a student. So the uniquely gifted and brilliant charismatic personality was a sinner, but would he be willing to admit it to those about him? He saw further that as regarding the Holy Spirit he must claim the promise for himself and then declare publicly that he had taken this step of faith that he might have the fullness of God's Spirit. This was a frightening step of faith. Now *everyone* would know what kind of man he was.

It was a meeting in a little mission house that precipitated the crisis. A lady was in charge and they were singing the song, "Touch Me Again, Lord." Chambers knew that his time had come. He must now act in obedience to God as he understood that Scripture. He arose to his feet and told them that on the basis of the Word of God he was claiming the promise of the fullness of the Holy Spirit and he was fulfilling the conditions by making this public declaration. Then he sat down. He said later that it was a painful experience, but what followed was "ten times worse." The lady, leading the meeting, misunderstood him and thought he did it as an example to others and said so. Chambers' response was to get to his feet and say, "I go up for no one's sake. Either Christianity is a downright fraud, or I have not got hold of the right end of the stick." Then and there, however, he renewed his claim on the promise of the gift of the Holy Spirit according to Luke 11:13.

Chambers was disappointed for it did not appear that God had kept His end of the bargain. There was no rending of the heavens or an inner witness to his soul. But later on in a meeting when he was speaking, 40 people responded to the invitation. This terrified him because he was still looking at himself and he was empty and dry as before. In his perplexity he went to his superior, Mr. McGregor, and told him what had happened. The principal then reminded him of how he had laid claim to the baptism of the Holy Spirit and that it would result in power, for Jesus had said, ". . .ye shall receive power. . ." At this point the inner witness was given. Realization came to his heart. He said later, "When you know what God has done for you, the power and tyranny of sin is gone." The previous four years that had been such a dreadful experience were now followed by five years of heaven upon earth. The last aching abyss of his heart was now filled to overflowing and Jesus was at the center of his find. Rest had at last come to this young pilgrim.

The years passed and Chambers seems to have left Dunoon around 1903. In the following years he traveled extensively, both at home and abroad. His message was the deeper life message that had so revolutionized his life. "It is no wonder," he said, "that I talk so much about an altered disposition: God altered mine. I was there when He did it, and I have been there ever since."

Chambers was a Baptist, but when he came to the Holiness camp meetings of our country he was able to write back to England and say, "These are my kind of people." In a Quaker home where he was staying it was "thee," "thou," and "thy." But he went on to add, "These saints have had experiences as I have of the two distinct works of grace, and I find the bonds of the Spirit are closer than anything I have ever known before."

Chambers was able to employ a wide spectrum of theological expression when it came to defining his deeper experience. He would call it the "filling of the Holy Spirit." When speaking to his friends, the Holiness people, he would employ such expressions as "sanctified," "entire sanctification," and "holiness." A term he often used, and which was very close to his heart, was "personal, passionate devotion to Jesus Christ."

The years of itinerant travel gave way to the more settled life in a Bible college. He had married Gertrude Hobbs in 1910, and in 1911 he was asked to become the principal of this newly-formed Bible school. The testimonies of gratitude from the students in later years show the high esteem in which he was held.

He was always an early riser, a man of prayer, a man of simple tastes, and a man who believed that the Sermon on the Mount was for our day. Even the evangelical world was hard pressed here. This sermon of Jesus seemed impossible in its demands. Not so, said Chambers. Students took issue with him, but he did not argue. Time and example would persuade them.

Chambers himself was a living example of the Sermon on the Mount. He taught that, if a life is rightly related to God and empowered with the Holy Spirit, the by-product of that union will be the Sermon on the Mount lived out in life. In years to come, the students, seasoned by time, experience, and memory, were to thankfully vouch for the reality of his teaching.

There was a facet of his personality that endeared him to his students and fellowmen. Whereas in his early student days he had been morose and severe, the opposite was now true. He had an engaging sense of humor. It is doubtful that he could have passed for the stereotyped parson.

The "sanctified," too, had a little difficulty here. One such person said, "On first coming in touch with the Reverend Oswald Chambers, I was shocked at what I considered his undue levity. He was the most irreverent reverend I had ever met." Then he added, "It was entirely due to my own ignorance concerning the experience of sanctification. . .he was true as steel to his Lord and master."[1]

Speaking of a later time in the Chambers' quarters on the YMCA compound in Egypt, the Reverend Douglas Downes wrote, "I remember a supper party taking place in one of its tiny rooms with such hilarity as might have shocked the respectably religious into believing what the Jews believed of the apostles on the day of Pentecost."[2]

The war brought with it many changes. By the year 1915 it was decided to close the college for the duration. Chambers felt impressed to join the YMCA, and later that same year he was assigned to work among the British troops in Egypt. There at the YMCA outpost they ministered to the material and spiritual needs of the troops. Later he was joined by his wife and four-year-old daughter, Kathleen.

It was a memorable time for them all. Chambers was at his best when speaking to these doughboys. He did not look upon them as "poor, dear men." His estimate of them, no doubt, had much to do with them being drawn to him. He was not a preacher of the sawdust trail. He had observed that the shallow type of Christian experience could not withstand the rigors of the battlefront. His discourses were deep and profound, but thoroughly Christ-centered. He was never satisfied until his listener was anchored to the Rock of Ages.

The lack of pious religiosity in his own life caused these hardened soldiers to be drawn to him. They sensed that this "apostle of the haphazard," so unconventional and different, had the key to the kingdom and was offering it to them. Whether it was Sunday services or midweek, come they did. They came where he was, and he was not above coming to where they were.

One such example stands out. It was the night of the concert and boxing match. As 1,200 men waited for the boxing to begin, who should climb under the ropes and into the ring but Chambers, who then proceeded to ask God's blessing on the event. He once said, "I never buttonhole them, but they do me, and make the most astonishing confessions and vows."

Then came the day of departure and back to the hut they went to bid "O.C." farewell. Most of them he never saw again. Some died on the battlefield, and before the rest could see him again he himself had been called to higher service. He had been assigned to General Allenby's forces then moving into the Judean hills toward Jerusalem. He was awaiting his final orders when he became severely ill. He rallied, but later died.

The one who made the invisible world so personal and real to those about him was seen once more. Mrs. Claude Pickens wrote:

One night as we were sitting on the deck of the American Mission Boat, the Ibis, talking about him, suddenly, to my astonished eyes, he appeared, seated on the corner of the table, as natural as ever, though seemingly more radiant. He said, "Bulger, let not your heart be troubled. It is all right. You can't understand God's ways, but get down into his love. Don't lose your grip, be radiant for him." I turned to Mrs. Chambers and asked, "Did you see him just now?" And though she had not seen him she believed me. The vision was real and is still vivid. . ."[3]

In the military cemetery in old Egypt lies the remains of this remarkable servant of God. A simple white headstone with an open Bible before it has this inscription on it: "A Believer in Jesus Christ."

[1]Oswald Chambers, *Oswald Chambers, His Life and Work*, p. 206.
[2]*Ibid*, p. 250.
[3]Chambers, p. 252.

12

Madam Guyon (1648-1717)

Catholic

She was probably one of the greatest women Europe ever produced. Yet few in her time really knew her, nor knew that her presence among them had been a time of divine visitation. Like her Master before her, she was despised and rejected, yet the imprint of her godly life is permanently embedded in the history of the Christian Church.

Madam Guyon was born in Montargis, France, in 1648 to members of the aristocracy. Her parents were highly regarded, wealthy, and religious. But it was their daughter who was destined to bring to her generation a personal religious lifestyle so rare, penetrating, and beautiful that it created discomfort among many, but hunger and hope in others.

There was little in her childhood to indicate the great spiritual contribution she was destined to make in her lifetime. She was frail, surrounded by wealth, cared for by servants and friends, and moved from place to place. Personal parental care, so important in child rearing, was minimal. Her education was likewise neglected, but when she was seven she was placed in the Ursuline Convent where her half sister took her under her special care, and the child made rapid progress "in learning and piety." At the age of eight she was placed in the Dominican Convent where she remained for eight months. Here she found a Bible, and became deeply absorbed in it. In her own words she says, "I spent whole days in reading it. And having great powers of recollection I committed to memory the historical parts entirely." Though she was yet young, the memorization of Scripture would be important in the future, for it would be a part of the foundation upon which God would do His work in her life.

Guyon's mental powers and knowledge of the Scriptures did not, however, bring her to faith and rest in God. Consequently her young life, like a pendulum, would swing from one extreme to another. For a period of time she would be wholly occupied in religious pursuits. She would visit the poor, give them food and clothing, and even instruct them in religious matters. At other times she would succumb to the enticements of a profligate age. Her beauty, love of fashions, and witty conversation drew her away from God. When her parents moved to Paris in 1663 they exposed their daughter to further temptation.

Paris was a pleasure-living city in a time of an evil Monarchical reign, that of Louis the 14th. It was here that she met her future husband, Jaques Guyon. She had no special love for him but because he was a man of wealth, her father "arranged" for their marriage to fit his wishes. She was now almost 17 and he was 38.

The new life upon which she was now to embark and remain for the next 17 years could only be described as catastrophic. It was a 17th century Job experience, only it extended over a longer period of time. This refined and sensitive woman was destined to die to everything of this world, but to rise amidst the ashes in such beauty as only a few could comprehend and appreciate. She had come to understand that God was in everything and was leading her by the hand. The world was His schoolroom, and He was personally tutoring her in preparation for her life's work.

Instead of happiness, the marriage arrangement became a "house of mourning." Her mother-in-law was a part of that arrangement. Unlike Guyon, she had little or no education, was loud and abusive, and a stranger to the refined sensibilities that characterized her beautiful daughter-in-law. Instead of the role of a live-in guest, she took the helm and ruled with an iron hand. Guyon's husband, ill much of the time, was influenced by his mother against his wife. Though he loved her, he was often unreasonable and angry with her.

To all appearances her marriage was a failure. Her earthly hopes were blasted. She did not yet see the hand of God in all of this. Later, however, she acknowledged, "Such was the strength of my natural pride, that nothing but some dispensation of sorrow would have broken down my spirit and turned me to God." She also prayed, "Thou hast ordered these things, oh my God, for my salvation. In goodness thou has afflicted me. Enlightened by the result, I have since clearly seen that these dealings of thy providence were necessary in order to make me die to my vain and haughty nature."

The order of God's arithmetic in our lives is to subtract before He can add. Guyon came to know this in all its fury and fullness. First there was the loss of much of their enormous wealth. This was not as great a problem to the young woman as it was to her avaricious mother-in-law. In her bitterness, life in the household became even more unbearable.

Then Guyon's health began to fail. This, however, she came to look upon as a blessing in disguise, because now she began to think more of spiritual things. A simple Franciscan monk was instrumental in leading her to understand the true basis for a right relationship with God. It was not by any works of her own, as she had supposed, but by simple faith in Jesus

Christ. His was the finished work, and it was for her. That was all she needed. She said, "I was all of a sudden so altered that I was hardly to be known, either to myself or others. I experienced joy unspeakable, I praised God with profound silence."

She was 20 when she received this definite assurance of salvation. Speaking to the Franciscan monk she said, "I love God more than the most affectionate lover among men loves the object of his earthly attachment." She lived in this euphoric state of mind for two years. Meditation, prayer, and serving others was her delight.

But on a trip to Paris all this changed. Her beauty, dress and witty conversation drew her immediately into the center of the Parisian social life. All of a sudden the mountaintop experience with God that she had been enjoying for the past two years was gone. Having "tasted of the world to come" she was devastated by the thought that she could so easily walk away from His presence.

This state of mind continued for three months. She now turned for help to her close friend and counselor, Genevieve Grainger, and to some books on the deeper Christian life by A. Kemps, Francis de Sales, and the life of Madam Chantal. Still her distress continued.

Then one day while walking across one of the bridges of the river Seine, in Paris, on her way to Notre Dame Church, she was joined by a poor man in religious garb. Almost immediately the conversation turned to spiritual things. She was amazed. This total stranger seemed to know everything about her. "This man," she said, "gave me to understand that God required not merely a heart of which it could only be said it is forgiven, but a heart which could properly, and in some real sense, be designated as holy, that it was not sufficient to escape hell, but that He demanded also the subjection of the evils of our nature, and the utmost purity and height of Christian attainment." She was deeply affected, for she sensed the message had come directly from God. From that day on she resolved to live wholly for Him and that, "The world shall have no portion in me."

Having given God the right-of-way in her life, the heavenly surgeon began doing His work. There were idols to be destroyed and purgings to be made.

She was a very beautiful woman, but her beauty had been a snare to her. Upon awakening one morning, she found she had been stricken with smallpox. When the illness had run its course, she asked for a mirror. On finding her beauty totally and completely destroyed, she thanked God for His faithfulness. Though she had lost her outward beauty, she found herself in a most tranquil frame of mind.

Other trials followed. Her youngest son, of whom she was especially fond, sickened and died. This was a great blow to her, but she was beginning to see the hand of God in her trials. Because of this she shed no tears at his death.

When she was 24 her father died, and that same year her three-year-old also died. Shortly thereafter Grainger died. Finally, her husband, who had been ill so much of their married life, died. Now, at the age of 28 and bereft of all earthly supports, she could yet look up and whisper, "Oh, the adorable conduct of my God."

Two years earlier, when Guyon was about 26, she had been ushered into yet another phase of her training. She called it "a state of privation or desolation." Others of her faith have called it the "dark night of the soul." This lasted for seven years. During this period she was without any conscious joy, peace or emotional uplift. She had to walk by faith alone. This was not easy. Her background and religious training had majored on good works. Her introspective nature did not help her. Studying her moods, feelings and emotions could only add to her feelings of depression.

In earlier years she had been instrumental in leading a Barnabite Priest, Father LaCombe, to peace with God. Now it was he who led her to a better understanding of God's dealings in her life. She had not been forsaken, as she had supposed. On the contrary, God was close at hand. It was He who was crucifying the self-life. In a most personal way He was polishing His vessel.

At last she began to see that she had been a captive of her feelings and emotions, and that God wanted her to live above these, on a plateau of faith. Guyon was now about 33, seasoned by time, hardship, and the dealings of the Holy Spirit. She had found the true way of salvation for herself and had begun to lead many others also to peace with God. Now she had further insight into the interior life of sanctification. Like salvation, it was obtained by faith.

Now being able to rest in Him, her soul was aflame with the power of the Holy Spirit. Multitudes flocked to her for help. Revivals followed her wherever she went. Soon the common man was seeking the deeper experience she was talking about. She called it, "victory over the self-life," "pure love," or "death to the self-life." She seems to have clearly understood that this was the work of the Holy Spirit.

The woman, who for a long time had thought that she had lost God forever, came into the forefront as a leader of spiritual renewal. Not only did she influence the common man, but many of the clergy as well. Priests and bishops began to spread abroad her teachings on the victorious Christian life. One of the names given the movement was "quietism." Like the Quakers of a later day, they would wait quietly before God for the promptings of His spirit before they took any action.

The spiritual renewal went beyond the borders of her own land and spread over all of Europe. The change in the people's lifestyle that followed in its wake was so great that it upset the social and religious life everywhere. Men and women abandoned their worldly ways and committed themselves wholly to God.

This came as an awful shock to priests and nominal

Christians who were professing Christians but in reality did not know God. Then the inevitable happened. The people involved in the renewal began to be persecuted. Father LaCombe went to prison and was cruelly tortured. Guyon also was imprisoned. During her incarceration her spiritual life came under scrutiny. The testings were severe, but she had learned how to suffer. Instead of crumbling under the ordeal, she prospered. She occupied herself in prayer, praise, and writing. These writings spread all over France and Europe and only furthered the ministry.

After an eight month incarceration she was released, but later was imprisoned again. Finally she was placed in France's notorious prison, the Bastile, where she remained for four years. But so sure was she of God's providence and care over her that, instead of being depressed, she was radiant for Him. Her prison cell seemed like a palace to her. There was no place for remorse or regrets. After all, her sole crime was that she loved God.

Guyon was about 54 when she was released from prison. In the remaining 15 years of her life she gave unselfishly of herself in God's service, ministering to the poor and needy. Not only were the people of her time the beneficiaries of her life and service, but posterity as well. Her prolific pen had produced no less than 60 volumes of writings. These have ministered to hungry hearts in every age and around the world. Her Christian philosophy of life is set forth in a little poem:

> "To me remains no place or time;
> My country is in every clime;
> I can be calm and free from care
> On any shore since God is there."[1]

[1]James Gilchrist Lawson, *Deeper Experiences of Famous Christians*, p. 104.

13

John Hyde (1865-1912)

Presbyterian

After the goodbyes had been said and the tears shed, the ocean liner slipped out to sea. The voyage to India would not be easy. Months would pass before they would reach their destination. The rookie missionary would have time to study, plan, and pray, for there would be much to do once he set foot on Indian soil. The normal ambitions and expectations of youth were his, too. God, of course, would work through him, and great things would be accomplished. Thus mused the young missionary candidate.

A few hours out of New York's harbor a letter was delivered to him. It had been sent in care of the ship. It was from a good friend of his father. How good to have friends who care, he might have thought, as he tore open the envelope and began to read.

Slowly he began to seethe with anger.

John Hyde, who was normally gentle and quiet, was, for the moment, out of character as he flung the missive onto the floor. Was the writer implying that he was not qualified to go to the mission field? In his mind he rehearsed his qualifications to himself. Had he not been accepted as a qualified candidate by the mission board? Was not his father one of the outstanding clergymen in and around Carthage (Illinois)? Was he not a preacher's kid and a college and seminary graduate? How did this "friend" have the audacity to suggest that he needed to receive the baptism of the Spirit if he was going to be able to render effective service in God's kingdom? Didn't John Hyde, the pastor's son, an orthodox Presbyterian, know that?

Finally, the storm within him subsided and his better judgment prevailed. He picked up the letter again and reread it. This man was not out to ridicule or belittle him. He wanted to be of help. Perhaps he did need something more than what he had. Slowly his anger was replaced by hunger. For the duration of the voyage he gave himself to prayer, seeking the fulfillment of the promise made by Jesus when he said, "Ye shall receive power, when the Holy Ghost is come upon you; and ye shall be witnesses both in Jerusalem and in all Judea and Samaria, and unto the uttermost parts of the earth."

Arriving at his destination, Hyde settled into his quarters on the compound and began his labors. First of all there was intensive language and Bible study. This was coupled with visitation work in the many villages.

The years rolled by, but there was little fruit from all his efforts. In addition, it seemed he got little cooperation from the Lord, for he was ill so much of the time. This revelation of need everywhere, and his helplessness to do much about it, hastened the demise of his self-sufficiency, and reinforced the growing conviction that only the power of God could accomplish the task of changing the hearts of men.

Hyde began to spend more and more time in prayer. He took the promises to God and answers came. He was learning to pray more effectively. Others were inspired by his prayer life and began to do likewise. In 1904 a group of missionaries formed the "Punjab Prayer Union." Those interested in becoming members were required to subscribe to the following five principles:

1. Are you praying for quickening in your life, in the life of your fellow workers, and the church?
2. Are you longing for greater power of the Holy Spirit in your own life and work, and are you convinced that you cannot go on without this power?
3. Will you pray that you may not be ashamed of Jesus?
4. Do you believe that prayer is the great means for securing this spiritual awakening?
5. Will you set apart one half hour each day as soon after noon as possible to pray for this awakening, and are you willing to pray until this awakening comes?[1]

Hyde was a part of this group from the beginning. Together they looked upon the great field of India and saw the whitened harvest field. They had now been there long enough and tried hard enough to know that unless there was divine guidance and implementation, there would be no harvesting. They remembered the words of Jesus: "Without me ye can do nothing." They also remembered the great commission and other promises, all calculated to ensure success in God's way and in His time.

There was born out of their praying a desire for a conference which came to be called the First Sialkot Convention. The purpose of the conference was to build up believers and to serve as a gospel thrust to the unsaved. Church life everywhere was far below the Bible standard. There seemed to be little knowledge of the work of the Holy Spirit, and consequently, few were being retrieved from among the lost.

The convention drew hundreds of people. Hyde, of course, was one of the leaders and teachers, yet he was much of the time in the background, waiting upon God in fasting and prayer. It was here that God dealt with him. Much of what happened in private would later be reflected in the public assembly. Hyde would acknowledge how God had been dealing with him regarding some sin or wrong attitude that stood in his way, whereupon the same conviction would grip the people.

Many years had now come and gone since that day aboard ship when Hyde had asked God to baptize him with the Holy Spirit. Growth and maturity had followed. One day a further dimension was added to his Christian experience. He was speaking to his fellow missionaries at the convention on the work of the Holy Spirit. While he was speaking, the Lord opened up to him the truth of sanctification, and he saw it, too, was obtained by faith just like salvation.

One morning, as Hyde was leading a Bible class, he was speaking on John 15:26, 27: "He shall bear witness of me." In developing the theme he said, "Is the Holy Spirit first in your pulpits, pastors? Do you consciously put Him in front and keep yourselves behind Him when preaching? Teachers, when you are asked hard questions, do you ask His aid as a witness of all Christ's life? He alone was a witness of the incarnation, the miracles, the death and the resurrection of Christ."

Hyde was led to ask God specifically for one soul a day, and by the end of the year over 400 had come to Christ. Later he was led to ask the Lord for two souls a day, and this, too, was granted. He then became bolder and asked for four souls a day. There were times when his faith was severely tried and tested, but by the end of the year God had granted his request.

The Sialkot conventions touched the lives of thousands of people. Great numbers of native pastors, teachers, and evangelists returned to their communities renewed and refreshed. They launched out on their own ministries with renewed vision. "I am assured," said one who was there, "that thousands have been born into the kingdom because of the soul travail at Sialkot. Myriads will one day rise up to thank God that two or three men in northern India in the name of Jehovah said, 'Let us have a convention at Sialkot.' "[2]

After less than 20 years in India Hyde's health no longer permitted him to continue. He returned home by way of England and went to visit friends in Wales. While there he heard that Dr. Wilbur Chapman and song leader Charles Alexander were holding services in Shrewsbury. Together with two friends he went to hear the evangelist and remained for several days. They enjoyed the services very much but sensed that something was wrong.

The turnout for the services was small and the results meager. As Hyde viewed the situation, the burden of prayer for Shrewsbury settled heavily upon him. Soon the tide turned and the hall was packed. At the close of the service 50 people responded to the invitation.

Chapman was so impressed that he sought out Hyde and asked him to pray for him. As they knelt in prayer five minutes elapsed before the missionary uttered a word, and then with tears streaming down his face all he could say was, "Oh God." Silence reigned for another five minutes. Finally, putting his arm over the evangelist's shoulder he began to pray. It was such a prayer as he had never heard before. "I arose from my knees," Chapman said later, "to know what real prayer was."

Hyde remained there for a week and then returned to Wales. The following day he was seriously ill, hardly able to speak, but he smiled and whispered, "The burden of Shrewsbury was very heavy, but my Savior's burden took him down to the grave."

Hyde, on his way home to Carthage, was hospitalized when he reached New York City. There it was determined that a malignant brain tumor was the cause of his illness. He died February 17, 1912.

Though his ministry in India lasted less than 20 years, he pioneered a way of life that God could bless. It was not the life of working for God, but rather learning to work with Him, under His leadership and direction.

[1]Frances McGaw, *Praying Hyde*, p. 21.
[2]McGaw, p. 60.

117

14

John Bunyan (1628-1688)

Baptist

"**M**r. Fixit" had grown up 'midst pots and kettles. From his father he had learned the art of mending household utensils. It was a lowly calling—the kind of work that was only fit for gypsies. Had he lived in a more sophisticated age he might have been called a "restoration engineer." Instead, he was known simply as a tinker. But this tinker was destined to leave his name on the honor roll of England's greatest sons. His influence would be felt around the world for all time.

It was John Bunyan, the pot mender, who would leave his mark as an author. One of his books in particular, *Pilgrim's Progress*, was destined to become a classic.

The descriptive allegory of a believer's journey in *Pilgrim's Progress*, from the time he is awakened to a sense of his sinfulness to the day he enters into the presence of the King, is probably without parallel in Christian literature. Its popularity was due to the fact that the reader so readily identified with the central character, Christian. The reader, like Christian, was on a journey. He, too, had heard about the impending destruction coming upon his city. He also knew there was a way of escape—an escape to a better land with a city so beautiful that it defied description. The fact that Christian got out of his country in time, overcame the many obstacles, routed his enemies, and finally arrived safely at the heavenly portals gave the reader hope and encouragement.

We would naturally think that a man who could bequeath to his and following generations such a rich legacy of helpfulness must have been a cultured and educated man. He was neither. In his own words he describes himself as coming from "a low and inconsiderable generation." He received some basic education, but left school at the age of 10 to begin his apprenticeship under his father.

From his earliest youth he seems to have been a law unto himself. In spite of the efforts of his parents to give him some religious training and guidance, he continued to deteriorate in morals and behavior. He once said he had but few equals for both cursing, swearing, lying, and blaspheming the name of God.

But the hand of God was upon Bunyan. The wickedness of the day gave way to remorse at night. His mind would take inventory and his conscience would sit in judgment. There would be fearful dreams and dreadful vision. Then came the thoughts of judgment and hell. This was the inner turmoil and consequent afflictions, not of a grown man, but of a boy who was not yet in his teens. Yet with the break of day the cycle would be renewed. He was, by his own admission, "a ring leader of all the youth that kept me company in all manner of vice and ungodliness."

Bunyan was only 20 when he married. His wife was a woman of unusually fine character and a member of the Anabaptist church. The Bunyans were extremely poor. Materially they had nothing. But they had each other and they had youth, strength, and hope on their side. They were sure their tomorrows would be better.

It was not too difficult to trace the thread of God's care over him. Twice Bunyan nearly drowned. Once he was nearly bitten by a poisonous adder. At another time a man took his place in the army and was killed while on sentinel duty.

There was another facet of God's providence which was equally important. His wife's father had been a godly man, and before his death he had bequeathed to his daughter two books: *The Plain Man's Pathway to Heaven* and *The Practice of Piety*. The young couple would often sit together and read from these books. These, plus a particular sermon preached by their pastor, had the effect of temporarily awakening them from their spiritual slumber.

The sermon, however, was soon forgotten, and he went back to his old ways. Conviction and remorse would each take their turn in pummeling their victim. He concluded that he had overstepped the bounds of God's care. He felt he was eternally doomed.

Since there was no more hope he gave vent to most outrageous behavior. He would take what he could from life, good or bad, before the lights went out.

A well-administered rebuke was leveled at him one day from a most unlikely source. A woman of the street whom Bunyan describes as a "loose and ungodly wretch" told him that his cursing, swearing and general behavior was such as to make her tremble and she further added that by his life and wayward actions he was in a position to ruin all the youth in the whole town.

After this well-merited rebuke, Bunyan resolved on a new course of action. He would quit his swearing, give up dancing, begin reading the Bible and start keeping the 10 commandments. And, of course, he would start attending church regularly.

The reformation was in stark contrast to his former way of life, and the neighbors could not help but notice it. The young man, too, seemed to be pleased with himself and his new role, but a role was all it was, and God has His way of dealing with play actors.

As Bunyan went from house to house mending pots and pans he overheard a small group of ladies talking about the things of God. At the moment their subject was the new birth. They seemed to be very happy, and furthermore, they seemed to know what they were talking about. Their confidence, assurance, and insight into what was the true Christian way of life thundered into the ears of the young hypocrite. He didn't understand much of what they said, but he understood enough to conclude that he was far from God. In a matter of moments the scaffolding of his religious life lay in shambles.

Seeing that he had never been born again, he set out in earnest to make his peace with God. The ladies offered to help him. They sent for their pastor, Mr. Gifford. Gifford pointed in the Scriptures to the gate of entrance and to Calvary. Yet faith is often hard to obtain. The seed of the Word must be sown and then allowed to take root before the blade shows above ground.

Though he had been told to claim the promises of God, he neglected to cling to them long enough so as to become established in them. Instead he became introspective and looked at the circumstances around him. This is how he came to land in the "slough of despond."

This wretched existence lasted for over a year. It was a time of struggling to better himself. He would read his Bible, pray, and keep the commandments. But God was not impressed. Peace and rest of soul would never be purchased with personal effort. Intermittently, there would be flashes of light, as some Scripture promise would come to mind. There was Luke 13:22-23: "Compel them to come in that my house may be filled," and "yet there is room." This warmed his heart for the moment. "The Lord," said Bunyan, "must have thought of me when He spoke these words."

At another time, while traveling in the country, another passage of Scripture took on a personal meaning for him. It was Colossians 1:20: "He hath made peace by the blood of the cross." The he adds, "Now I could see that God and my soul were made friends by the blood of Jesus."

There were other times when, in his despair, Bunyan would lament and cry out that his only equal in wickedness was the devil himself. But these times of distress gradually gave way to a more permanent and complete rest in God.

This facet of his experience is set forth in the allegory when Christian enters in at the Wicket gate and comes to a place which he is unable to account for. The burden he has been carrying drops from his back and disappears.

Bunyan was now about 27. He had reached an important milestone in his Christian experience, but there were other battles yet to be fought. There were mountains to be scaled. There were giants yet to be dealt with. His faith would have to be enlarged and tested if he was to fulfill the calling that God had for him. There were several thoughts that still plagued him. Had he really been called of God? Was he among the elect? Might he not have sinned against the Holy Spirit and thus be lost forever? One by one these disturbing questions were defused as some appropriate Scripture gained the ascendency over his unbelief.

It was the sin of unbelief that had constantly dogged his footsteps and throttled his Christian witness. But one day he gained a great victory. While out walking in a field his eyes were opened as the words, "Thy righteousness is in heaven," bore down upon him. He was completely set free in an instant. "Now," he said, "did my chains fall off my legs indeed; I was loosed from my afflictions and irons; my temptations also fled away. . .now I went home rejoicing for the grace and love of God." In that moment Bunyan's Christian, like the Alpine climber, had peered over the top of the last mountain and there beheld Immanuel's land (also called the land of Beulah). It was beautiful, exceeding anything he had ever seen before.

Bunyan, for the first time, had begun to comprehend his union with Jesus Christ. Not only did he understand that Christ had died on the cross for him, but also that everything that happened to Christ had consequently happened to him, for the Savior's role had been one of substitution. If Christ had died and risen again, so had Bunyan. If the Lord was now seated at the right hand of the Father, so was Bunyan. He found the victory over self, sin, death, and the devil that he had sought for so long. He realized the victory had been procured for him through Jesus Christ. It left him in a state of euphoria. He was now the happiest of men. He began to share what God had done for him.

Having ascended to this plateau of faith he now became a powerful instrument for God in Christian service. He was not without conflicts, but now he knew what to do. Now he looked to God instead of himself. Victory was his by faith, and he held the banner high so others could see.

Before long he was preaching, and soon multitudes hung on his every word. Even the learned and educated came to hear him. One prominent clergyman, Dr. Owen, loved to hear him preach. When asked by King Charles II why he would listen to the illiterate tinker, the minister replied, "I would gladly give up all my learning for the tinker's power of preaching."

Great numbers of people were converted under his ministry, but there were others who took offense at his plain preaching. These ferreted out an old English law which forbade anyone to hold services separate from the Church of England.

The charge against him read as follows: "John Bunyan, of the town of Bedford, laborer, hath devilishly and perniciously abstained from coming to church to hear Divine Service, and is a common upholder of several unlawful meetings and conventicles, to the great disturbance and distraction of the good subjects of this kingdom, contrary to the laws of our Sovereign Lord the King."

Since Bunyan, then 32, would not cease his preaching he finally went to prison. He could have been released upon promising to obey the authorities, but he assured them, "If you let me out today, I will preach tomorrow." Twelve years went by. The jailer, however, was good to him, allowing him to read, write and visit his family from time to time.

But Bunyan grieved over his loved ones and was especially burdened for his little blind daughter. With the father in prison who would care for them? His refusal to obey the magistrates was not because he was obstinate, but he was afraid he might deny Christ. "If I give up preaching," he said, "I shall be considered a traitor to Christ in the day of judgment."

Bunyan was released from prison in the fall of 1672. He was 44. Shortly after his release, he became the pastor of the Bedford church, but in addition was in demand as a preacher all over England.

When he was 47 he was again imprisoned for a time. It was during this period, with only his experiences, the Bible, and *Fox's Book of Martyrs* that he wrote his immortal work— *Pilgrim's Progress*. The work was completed and published shortly after his release from the Bedford jail. Only 10 more years remained before his death at age 60.

15

Charles Grandison Finney (1792-1875)

Congregational

The little one-room schoolhouse had, for the occasion, become a church sanctuary. There was no pulpit, but the young missionary didn't need one. Trained in the arena of law, he roamed the front and up and down the aisle. It was an unforgettable sight to see this young man plead the cause of Christ. His sincerity and earnestness no one could doubt, and when he looked at the people with those eyes, often with tears rolling down his cheeks, he planted the seeds of sorrow and terror in their hearts for the way they had treated their Savior.

An old supreme court judge once gave him some sage advice that was destined to play an important role in his future ministry. "Charlie," he said, "you win a legal case by telling it simply, repeating it as many times as there are men in the box. Tell it simply and never read it."[1]

Charles Grandison Finney was born in Warren, Connecticut, on August 29, 1792. His father, Sylvester Finney, had fought in the Revolution and after the war settled down and became a farmer. Later they moved to the southern shore of Lake Ontario. This became their permanent home.

Finney learned early the value of hard work. There were the farm chores, felling of logs, and soil to be tilled. But it wasn't all work. There were the times when he would take his double-barreled flintlock and roam the woods looking for deer, turkeys, and pigeons. He was an excellent marksman. He seems to have always applied himself well in whatever he undertook. This was true of his work, recreation, or school.

School seasons were summer and winter, leaving the students free for the farm work in spring and fall. By the age of 16 he was considered sufficiently advanced to begin teaching.

The curriculum was simple in those days. . .reading, writing, and arithmetic. The qualifications for a teacher were that he knew "how to read correctly, spell accurately, write legibly, and keep the family accounts in order." It was customary for the families to take turns hosting the teacher, usually a week at a time.

Finney seems to have made out quite well in the schoolroom. In addition, he was a superb physical specimen. He excelled as an athlete, and the students loved him for it. Years later a grandson gave a descriptive word picture of his famous grandfather in his youth: "When he was 20," he said, "he excelled every man and boy he met in every specie of toil or sport. No one could throw him, no man could knock off his hat; no man could run faster, jump farther, leap higher or throw a ball with greater force or precision. When his family moved to the shores of Henderson's Bay near Sackets Harbor, he added to his accomplishments rowing, swimming, and sailing."[2]

Finney's teaching career was interrupted a couple of times when he returned to New England to attend high school "for a season." He seems to have had the equivalent of two years of high school training. During this time he became conversant in Latin, Hebrew, and Greek. In addition, he became quite proficient in music, learning "to read music at sight and to play the cello."

Finney was ambitious to get on in the world. He thought about attending Yale. But in the end he decided to study law under Judge Benjamin Wright in Adams, only 12 miles away. He was a diligent student as he read and pondered Blackstone's and other law books. By the end of the first year he had a small clientele, and a year later he was a partner in the law office.

In order to move ahead in life he must become a mason, his peers argued. And so he did. His stature in the community would be enhanced (it might even be profitable) if he belonged to some church. So this spiritually ignorant heathen from the backwoods, who was so completely innocent in matters spiritual, was corraled and given a baton so he could lead the church choir. If he were to be the choir director he *had* to be in church, and if he were in church he would *have* to listen to the preacher.

It was hard to swallow everything that he heard from the pulpit. The minister, an educated man and considered orthodox, seemed to assume that all those listening to him were theologians. In addition, in the estimate of the young lawyer, his logic was horrible. . .and he told him so. As an attorney, Finney was accustomed to presenting his arguments in a reasonable and logical sequence so as to convince a jury. He was not greatly impressed when the preacher would speak on the necessity of personal repentance and then conclude that such was not possible for man. God would have to do it. The end result was that people were waiting for God to convert them.

The minister, Rev. Gale, was anxious to know what progress was being made with his young choir director, so he made it a point from week to week to talk with him. There was much at stake. He knew that this young man was an important key to reaching others, especially young people. And Gale would customarily ask Finney for his opinion on his sermons. Instead of pampering the pastor's ego, the young man spoke his piece. Sometimes these became heated arguments. Gale finally concluded that there was little hope for Finney. What was worse was the hold Finney had on the young people. Many of them were in danger of being ruined, Gale reasoned, and even went so far as to warn the people against Finney.

But it wasn't all that bad. Some of these young people knew God and were praying for their choir director, his future sweetheart among them. Others in the church were praying, too. Faith might not be high, but they were praying.

An incident that occurred at the midweek prayer meeting jolted everyone. Some of the church members had been badgering Finney, asking if they should pray for him. Finney was not impressed. He acknowledged that perhaps he needed prayer but he reminded them that he did not think that their prayers had much virtue or were very effective. If they had been, surely the devil would have been driven out of Adam by now. So as far as prayer for a religious revival was concerned, Finney reasoned that to all appearances there was little hope for there was little faith for it.

The praying, preaching, and other people's concern, did do something. It created distress in the man's heart, and drove him to the Bible.

It was the fall of 1821. Finney was 29. His law practice had prospered and things were looking up. There was only one problem; his inner peace had not kept pace with his outward prosperity. If anything, there seemed to be a storm building up within the bosom of this young man.

One Sunday night Finney entered into a covenant with himself. He would avoid business as far as possible and tend to the matter of his soul's salvation. Fortunately for him, there was not much activity in the office the early part of that week which enabled him to spend his time reading the Bible and praying. When someone did come in he hurriedly covered up the Bible with other books so as not to arouse any suspicion that he might be concerned about his soul. He plugged the keyhole in the door for fear that someone would see him praying. When he finally saw the pride in his heart, it only added to his distress.

The following Monday and Tuesday were spent in huddle with his conscience. The horizon was growing darker. His convictions increased. In spite of his reading and searching he said later, "My heart grew harder. I could not shed a tear; I could not pray." By Tuesday night he was very nervous. What if he should die? "I knew if I did I should sink down into hell," Finney said.

The following morning he left early for the office. Just before arriving there an inward voice seemed to say to him, "What are you waiting for? Did you not promise to give your heart to God? What are you trying to do? Are you endeavoring to work out a righteousness of your own?"

In that moment the whole scheme of God's salvation opened up to his mind in a most remarkable manner. He saw the reality of God's finished work. The atonement of Christ was complete and could not be added to. Gospel salvation was a provision from God in heaven, and it only hinged on man's acceptance to make it operative. It was a gift without charge and without cost.

That morning Finney saw something of the depravity of man who would look askance at God's goodness, and in stupidity inquire, "What is the hitch?" All this time he had been standing in the middle of the road, transfixed, when the voice began to speak to him again. "Will you accept it now, today?" He replied, "Yes, I will accept it today, or I will die in the attempt."

Finney had been in the habit of taking daily walks into a wooded area north of town as weather permitted. Though it was a chilly October morning, he headed for the woods again. There would be no one to disturb him, he told himself. "I will give my heart to God, or I never will come down from there."

As he tried to hide away among the trees and bushes, he found his heart would not pray. He was on the verge of despair, when he discovered that it was his pride that stood in his way.

Now he was overwhelmed when he saw his wickedness. To think that a man should be ashamed to be found praying to God. The awful realization caused him to cast off all restraint and address the Lord at the top of his voice, not caring what anyone thought. Just at this point a passage of Scripture came to mind, "Then shall ye go and pray unto me and I will hearken unto you. Then shall ye seek me and find me when ye shall search for me with all your heart" (John 29:13). He laid hold of this promise instantly. He saw something he had never seen before. He had had an intellectual faith in the Word of God, but now he saw that true faith was a matter of the heart. It was a voluntary trust. . .not just an intellectual state.

Soon he was so full of joy he could hardly contain himself. It had not occurred to him that this was his conversion experience, but what he had tasted of the world to come made him promise, "If I am ever converted, I will preach the Gospel."

As he left the woods he discovered that it was already midday. Time had gone by so rapidly. One thing bothered him, though. He was no longer convicted about his sins. Try as he would, he was unable to conjure up any concern for his spiritual welfare.

That afternoon was spent moving furniture and books to another office. They were so busy there was little time for conversation, for which Finney was glad. His mind was in another world, and the tranquility that he was experiencing he would never be able to explain to his partner anyway.

That evening he decided to remain at the office where he could be alone. He would do some praying. After all, he had promised God he would make his peace with Him or die trying. He went into a room back of the front office where he could then pray and seek God. Though the darkness had already set in, the room seemed perfectly light. As he shut the door after him, he turned and seemed to come face to face with Jesus Christ. The Lord looked at him, but said nothing. Finney fell on the floor before Him, and wept like a child, making such confessions as he was able to. As an old man recalling and recording this experience, he wrote, "It did not occur to me then, nor did it for some time afterwards, that it was wholly a mental state."

Later he returned to the front office and noticed how much time had passed as he saw the fire he had built earlier in the evening was now reduced to ashes. As he was about to sit down by the fireplace he "received a mighty baptism of the Holy Ghost." It was so unexpected; such a thing had not even entered his mind. He spoke of the experience as being like a wave of electricity passing through him, or like "waves and waves of liquid love." Finally, he cried out, "I shall die if these waves continue to pass over me. . .Lord, I cannot bear anymore." Nevertheless, these waves continued for some time.

It was late in the evening when one of his choir members stopped by the office to see him. Finding the choir master in such a state of loud weeping he inquired, "Mr. Finney, what ails you?" Getting no coherent response, he again asked, "Are you in pain?" Finally Finney was able to say, "No, but so happy that I cannot live."

He tried to sleep that night, but time and again he was awakened by the surge of God's love flowing through him. Finally, towards morning, he was able to get some sustained sleep. When he awakened the sunshine flooded his room. Again, as during the night, the mighty baptism bathed his soul, but this time the Spirit seemed to be gently rebuking him. "Will you doubt?" to which he responded, "No, I will not doubt; I cannot doubt."

With such an initiation rite, the Spirit began to teach him. His "log cabin seminary" was elementary in the extreme. For not only did he have much to learn, but he had to fend off all kinds of heretical teaching, even though it came from his orthodox Presbyterian teacher, Gale. Gale was grateful in later years that he had not succeeded in molding Finney as he had sought to do. Finney, by his obstinacy, had provided the necessary correction to Gale's theology. Gale came to the conclusion that he, himself, had never been converted. Finney's controversies with Gale drove him to prayer and to seek out the answers from the Fountain Head Himself. This proved to be a great blessing. He would have formidable opposition in years to come, and at times would have no one to turn to but the Lord.

Finney's ministry began in a most inauspicious manner. A women's mission society sent him out as a missionary for six months. The thrust was to the more remote areas of the county. He held his services in schoolhouses and small churches. His strategy was to preach the Gospel, to explain it carefully so everyone understood, and to call for a decision. This was a new innovation. They were not accustomed to this, so when they did not respond they came under terrible condemnation, and they became angry with the evangelist. But his approach worked. Soon conviction, anger, and fear gave way to repentance and a living trust in God. The people became happy as they abandoned their old ways for the new way with God.

From this modest beginning the revival began to grow. Its tenacles not only reached into the remote frontier, but also into the cities. The man who felt that he was qualified to preach only in out-of-the-way places was now reaching the elite and sophisticated in the larger churches of the land.

For nine years this work went on. They speak of it as "The Saga of the Nine (golden) Years." There was the revival that came to Rochester, New York, in 1830-31.

The place was shaken to its foundations; 1,200 persons united with the churches of the Rochester Presbytery; all the leading lawyers, physicians, and businessmen became Christians; forty of the converts entered the ministry; the whole character of the town was changed.[3]

132

As a result of what happened in Rochester, revivals broke out in 1,500 towns and villages. But the pace was too fast, the demands made upon him too great. His health began to fail and he realized he would have to conserve his strength. Yet there were even greater days ahead. There were the Evangelistic Campaigns in the British Isles, and at home the burgeoning college and seminary at Oberlin. There, as head of the theology department, he was able to fashion preachers and evangelists to his own liking. He loved this work. The students loved him, and looked up to him, and he left his imprint upon all of them.

It was Sunday morning in the late '80s in San Jose, California, when "Pentecost fell at the earnest words of the minister." After the service a stranger approached the pastor and said, "You're a Finney man, aren't you?" With tears in his eyes the minister said, "Yes, thank God! I'm one of the thousand other lights."

Finney was originally identified with the Presbyterian church, but in 1833 he became a Congregationalist. The reason he gave was that it gave him more elbow room. He had come to call the anointing for service "entire consecration," although he also used terms such as the "baptism with the Holy Spirit" and "entire sanctification." He attributed the success of his ministry to the power of the Spirit upon him, and when this power was missing he would fast and pray, and usually by the day's end the anointing would be there again.

This blessed man was privileged to help mold a generation for God, but it didn't stop there. That generation produced another generation, and his two books, his biography, and his *Revival Lectures* have, from one generation to another, stirred the dying embers of spiritual life in the churches and mission stations around the world.

---

[1]Richard Ellsworth Day, *Man of Like Passions*, p. 54.
[2]Basil Miller, *Charles G. Finney*, p. 10.
[3]Day, p. 79.

16

Frances Ridley Havergal (1836-1879)

Church of England

Her name belongs in Christian history books if for no other reason than that she stirred the embers of song, so that British and Americans might better sing the songs of Zion. She also left a legacy of devotional reading for the benefit and blessing of the pilgrims on their way to the heavenly city. But besides song, books, and personal ministry is the record of an encounter with God that made her stand tall with both God and man.

Frances Ridley Havergal was born in 1836. She was raised in a Christian home, the youngest of six children. Her father was a clergyman of the Church of England. She was a very active and beautiful child, and her mental alertness was outstanding. She was able to read the Bible when she was only four years old. As a child she would sit on her father's knee and sing, and he would read to her from the Scriptures.

When she was six years old she heard a sermon on the terrors of hell and judgment day. Frightened, she told no one about it, but sought relief in prayer. When she finally got up enough courage to speak to someone about her distress, she came to the wrong person. The undiscerning curate listened and then counseled her by telling her to "be a good girl and pray." This she had already tried but found no relief. The disappointed child retreated to her own little world and tried to fend off the arrows of torment and fear.

It was a terrible time for Havergal. The surroundings about her grew darker. Her mother died when she was only 12. The distress and sorrow that now engulfed the little child can only be imagined.

A year or two later, however, it was her good fortune to be enrolled in a school conducted by Mrs. Tweed, a godly woman filled with the Spirit of God. She was one of those rare jewels who was not only concerned that the children under her care should learn the three R's, but that their spiritual welfare should be tended to as well. To this end she lived, prayed, and taught her charges, and soon she had a revival on her hands. Before long, more of her scholars had committed themselves to Christ, and their faces radiated their new found joy and peace.

Havergal, however, had not found relief. She had never ventured forth to seek help from anyone since that unfortunate day when she had opened her heart to the local clergyman. But she decided to try again. She came to her teacher, Miss Cook, and confided that she would be willing to give up everything and do anything if only she could find Christ as her Savior. This lovely woman, who later was to become her stepmother, spoke only a few words, but they were like salve on an open wound: "Why cannot you trust yourself to the Savior at once?" said Cook. Like the dark night that finally must give way to the sunrise, so the cloud lifted from her tortured mind.

"Yes, why not?" she thought. She ran home to think it over. On her knees in her room she pondered the new revelation.

She was held in the grip of joy for the realization of the truth was unfolding before her, of course she could trust Him. . .for all eternity. Then and there she made her commitment. It was final and it would be irrevocable. Now peace had come to her heart for she realized that He was worthy of her trust.

Havergal obtained a splendid education and became a "beautiful and accomplished lady." Her school years were spent in England and Europe. She mastered a half dozen languages, became proficient as a musician, singer, and writer. Though learning came easy for her, the educational institutions of Europe did not provide the best climate for character building or true spiritual development. It was the beginning of the era of rationalism. The institutions of higher learning were hotbeds of infidelity, and everyone who had the courage to stand up for his Christian convictions might have to stand alone. Out of a class of 110 ladies, she was the only truly converted one. But she stood her ground amidst opposition and ridicule, and in doing succeeded in winning some of her schoolmates to Christ.

At the age of 18 she returned to England. It was about this time that she was confirmed in Worcester Cathedral. With the laying on of hands the bishop prayed, "Defend, oh Lord, this child with thy heavenly grace, that she may continue thine forever and daily increase in the Holy Spirit, more and more until she come into thy everlasting Kingdom."[1]

Of this experience she said, "If ever my heart followed a prayer, it did then. If ever I thrilled with earnest longing not unmixed with joy, I did at the words 'thine forever.' "[2] In the years that followed, this anniversary day was always set aside and spent in prayer and "holy retirement."

Her services were now more and more in demand. There were Sunday School classes to be taught. Her gift of song was eagerly sought after. Then there were the poor to be visited and ministered to. When time permitted she would write, and before long these writings began to gain attention.

From the time of her conversion she had lived a wholly committed and consistent Christian life. This life had been nurtured and sustained by her study of the Word. She had always been an excellent student in school, and she was equally diligent in the study of the Bible. By the time she was 22 she had memorized the Gospels, Epistles, Revelation, Psalms and Isaiah.

However, in spite of her gifts, achievements, and consistent Christian behavior, she was not completely satisfied. There was a current of unrest inspired by the Holy Spirit to draw her on to experience God's provision for the "overcomer." No amount of earnestness, effort, Bible study, prayer, or Christian service had been able to alleviate this distress in her heart. In her book, *Gleams and Glimpses*, written in 1858, she writes: "Oh to be filled with joy and the Holy Ghost." At another time she laments, "Oh, why cannot I trust Him fully." And still later she cries out, "Oh that He would indeed purify me and make me white at any cost."

Let the reader observe her error, for we are all in this together. She was asking God for something that had already been provided. She continued asking, day by day and year by year, for at least 15 years. If, instead, she had simply brought her petition before God, and then continued to thank Him for the answer, the reality would have been transferred to consciousness much earlier, and her joy would have been complete. In all fairness to her we must say she did not struggle as some do, but she did say, "I still wait for the hour when I believe He will reveal Himself to me more directly; but it is the quiet waiting of present trust, not the restless waiting of anxiety and danger." It was her tarrying and waiting for the experience to be fulfilled in the future, instead of accepting it in the present here and now, that was the deceptive flaw in her thinking. What could have been hers, when she was first awakened to her need at 22, she did not realize until she was 37. . .only six years before she died.

137

Havergal was often mystified as to why others entered into this deeper experience with God so easily, when she had agonized and prayed so long and nothing had happened. She suspected it was her unbelief, but she made another observation. In her perplexity she reasoned that perhaps God was letting her experience trial, so that her sweet song might bring comfort to someone else in distress. It wasn't that God's smile of approval was on the years of unbelief, but we do learn from our mistakes and are seasoned by them. He has a way of taking us where we are, and just as we are, and making our lives redemptive. "I will restore to you the years that the locust hath eaten" (Joel 2:25).

Havergal was not a strong person. She had a continual bout with illness. It was for this reason that she traveled a good deal. She would often be found hiking in the mountains of Switzerland to help strengthen her frail body. When she was at home she was often prevented from attending conventions and conferences for the same reason. Consequently, the teachings of men played a minor role in her Christian development. Instead, she had learned to lean that much harder on God and His Word.

One day the promise of better days ahead stood at her doorway. It was the postman, and he had a package. It was a book, a small one, entitled, *All For Jesus*. She read it, and she was thrilled. It portrayed to her a fuller and more abundant Christian experience than she had yet experienced. But she had questions, and the full realization was still out there somewhere. She wrote to the author acknowledging her deep desire to know Jesus better, and believing that it was not doctrine she needed, but rather a fuller sense of "being with Him." She must have treasured the letter that came by return mail.

With a few strokes of the pen the writer had brought her to the top of the mountain range from which she could view God's promised land. It was beautiful. The ray of light and realization came to her when he quoted the verse, "The blood of Jesus Christ His Son cleanseth us from all sin'' (I John 1:7). It was the word ''cleanseth'' that opened her eyes and set her free. With rapturous voice she burst forth, ''I see it and I have the blessing.'' The young lady who had lamented ''Oh, why cannot I trust Him fully?'' now laments for another reason, ''Why should we pare down the promises of God?''

The sustaining power of this experience was tested when the American publishers of her writings went bankrupt in the financial crisis of 1873. This could have been a bitter blow to her if it had occurred just two months earlier. Instead it became a measuring stick for testing her new found experience with God. Fortunately she passed with flying colors. She had lost much of her potential royalties, but she had found God faithful and true to His promises, and this outweighed everything. She was able to say, ''It was worth it all.''

The closing years of her life were busy years. Her sister says, ''She literally wore herself out ministering to others.'' She was in pain much of the time, but she had a simple explanation for pain, a simple philosophy. ''Pain,'' she said, ''is no mystery when looked at in the light of God's holiness, and in the light of Calvary. Pain as to God's own children, is truly and really, only a blessing in disguise. It is but His chiseling, one of His graving tools, producing the likeness to Jesus for which we long. I never yet came across a suffering (real) Christian who could not thank Him for pain.''[3]

In her quest for a more satisfying walk with God we find this child of the Church of England using such terminology as ''true consecration,'' ''cleansed from all sin,'' ''made holy,'' ''entire sanctification,'' and ''the blessing.''

In 1873, the year in which she received her first glimpse of the ''land of Beulah,'' she wrote one of her great consecration hymns. From her book, *Kept for the Master's Use*, we find this beautiful poem which was later put to music:

> Take my life, and let it be
> Consecrated, Lord, to Thee.

139

Take my moments and my days
Let them flow in ceaseless praise.

Take my hands, and let them move
At the impulse of Thy love.

Take my feet, and let them be
Swift and "beautiful" for Thee.

Take my voice, and let me sing
Always, only, for my King.

Take my lips, and let them be
Filled with messages from Thee.

Take my silver and my gold;
Not a mite would I withhold.

Take my intellect, and use
Every power as Thou shalt choose.

Take my will and make it Thine;
It shall be no longer mine.

Take my heart; it is Thine own;
It shall be Thy royal throne.

Take my love; my Lord, I pour
At Thy feet its treasure-store.

Take myself, and I will be
Ever, only, all for Thee.

Havergal had just completed revising her latest book, *Kept for the Master's Use*, when she died on June 3, 1879. In her closing hours when her friends were trying to sympathize with her in her pain, she simply whispered, "Never mind! It's home the faster! God's will is delicious. He makes no mistakes."

Inscribed on her tomb at her request are the words: "THE BLOOD OF JESUS CHRIST CLEANSETH US FROM ALL SIN."

[1] J. Gilchrist Lawson, *Deeper Experiences of Famous Christians*, pp. 315-316.
[2] *Ibid*, p. 316.
[3] V. Raymond Edman, *They Found the Secret*, pp. 74-75.

17

Hans Nielsen Hauge (1771-1824)

Lutheran

That a Norwegian farmhand should take upon himself some of the duties of a Christian minister was unheard of. That he should succeed where most ministers had failed was even more alarming.

Hans Nielsen Hauge did both. With a fresh and pointed word from the Lord he startled sinners, and in the process incurred the wrath of the clergy. "This very remarkable man of God," says a historian, "was sent to Norway when he was needed the most, but whom the clergy wanted the least."[1]

Intrusion upon the enemy's domain, however, was costly. His evangelistic career was cut short and he spent years in prison.

Life in an unheated cubicle with poor food and little exercise had taken its toll. In the ordeal he had lost his teeth, his hair, and almost lost his faith. He learned first hand that when you are on an errand for God, bringing the message of relief to captives, there is a price to be paid.

Hauge was born April 3, 1771, in a community known as Tune Parish, about 50 miles from Oslo. His father was a well-to-do farmer. Both his parents were intelligent and godly people. They had a large family, members of which were exceptionally talented. At an early age Hauge showed promise of being the most gifted of all.

During his early years he acquired a working knowledge of carpentry, blacksmithing, bee culture, trading and, of course, farming. Later he became assistant to his brother who was the sheriff of the district.

But this bent for business did not absorb all his attention. He had had several near brushes with death so he was especially cognizant of the uncertainty of life. He spent a great deal of time pondering the great issues of the hereafter, and then there was the inevitable question always dogging his footsteps, was he ready to meet God?

Hauge declined entirely to take part in the amusements of the day, and because of this he was considered strange. Much of his spare time was spent reading and browsing among the books in his home. Fortunately, his parents had provided the family with a library of good reading. There was the Bible from which the family read every day. In addition there were books by Luther, Muller, the works of Pontoppidan, Collins, and Brorson. It is believed that he also had access to some of the writings of Johann Arndt, among them "True Christianity." Another book that was to influence him greatly was the biography of John Tauler.

John Tauler was a 14th century Dominican Friar and theologian. He was considered the greatest preacher of his time. Multitudes gathered from Sabbath to Sabbath to hear Tauler preach in the great cathedral in Strassburg. Despite his ability as an orator, he did not know God, and a simple Waldensian layman by the name of Nicholas of Basil told him so. Once he was convinced that this humble lay brother was right, he left his pulpit for two years to seek God for himself.

When Tauler returned to the Cathedral he was a different man. His preaching produced terrible conviction and men began to find their way back to God under his ministry.

It was this biography and sermons by Tauler that made a profound impression upon Hauge. In days to come he would be cast in a similar role. He was not the formally educated man that Tauler had been. Instead he was but a simple farmer with no more than the equivalent of a fourth grade education. But he was destined to rouse and shake the people of Norway from their spiritual slumber.

A brief look into Norway's history will help us to understand why. Norway had not really been touched by the Reformation. With the death of the last male descendents of the reigning dynasty in 1319, Norway gradually came under the control of Denmark.

For the next 500 years Norway's destiny was in the hands of a foreign power. This meant that Danish pastors were imported to care for the spiritual needs of the people. The arrangement was far from ideal. There was a great gulf between the pastor and his flock. It is said, "They had nothing in common. They never mingled socially. The minister was a superior person and the parishioner a subject, and to make matters still worse the minister was a foreigner who spoke a language the parishioners hardly understood.[2] The fact that he drew his salary from the state only made matters worse.

The system continued to foster the chasm between pastor and people. It further attracted men into the ministry who were not called to it. They had no spiritual sensitivity for the cause of God or the needs of the people. Though there were good men among them, the greater number did not belong in the ministry.

It was these men that were threatened when Hauge appeared so they purposed to stop him if possible. Though they could not lead a man to peace with God or send him on his way to heaven, they knew how to crank up the rumor mill. This vagabond farmer was, they said, a great threat to any community. He was a false prophet, a thief, a drunkard, and an adulterer.

But these were their problems, not his. Drunkenness was a great problem among them. In one case the parishioners complained to their superior about their minister, whereupon the delinquent pastor was advised that he would have to try and remain sober one day a week or they would have to remove him. Bishops themselves ridiculed Christianity and the pastors echoed their sentiments.

Because of the deplorable spiritual climate it would have been difficult for anyone to envision the great blessing God had in store for Norway. But He *was* at work. The instrument was being molded and prepared. The days of reading, studying and praying were part of that preparation. Finally it all converged and came into focus in an extraordinary experience when Hauge was called, commissioned and invested with the authority to carry it out.

He was working in his father's field and humming an old song. "Now," said he, "my heart was lifted up to God in such a way, I simply cannot explain it. There was a glory in my soul that no tongue could describe, something supernatural, divine, and blessed. I felt a most fervent love of God and my neighbor. My heart was completely changed."

While in this frame of mind he began to pray about God's will for his life. The experience of the prophet Isaiah came to mind when he was called to serve God. Echoing the words of the man of God he said, "Here am I, send me." Then the voice of the Spirit said to him over and over again, "You shall go east, west, north and south and confess my name before men. You shall exhort them to be converted from darkness to light."

A historian speaks of this experience as both his conversion and baptism with the Holy Spirit, but another biographer contends that Hauge was not converted suddenly. Yet a sudden transformation did take place in his inner life. His struggle, he said, had not been that between faith and doubt, but between willingness and unwillingness to follow God's call. However, both agree that the man was genuinely converted and also empowered and filled with the Holy Spirit. One writer says of this particular experience, "This was rightly called Hauge's spiritual, his Pentecostal, baptism."[3]

The young farmer's heart was now ablaze within him. But how could he share with others the euphoric Christian experience that had become his? Perhaps he could begin with his own family. His brothers and sisters, they would listen, he reasoned. Soon all were converted to Christ.

The effect Hauge had upon the people was astonishing. Such power attended these private conversions that a spiritual awakening was soon under way and gaining momentum. No less than 10 of his converts, two of them being his own brothers, became lay evangelists in their own right and came to be called the "teacher of Smaalenene," named after their own community.

The joy of ministering and seeing people converted to Christ was tempered by vicious rumors that Hauge was a "crazy fanatic," but it did not deter him from his soul winning.

These converts, with a new song in their hearts, stood in bright contrast to the rest of the community. Their liberating testimonies awakened many to the consciousness of their sins. The result was vehement opposition, but it was also the beginning of a great ingathering of souls.

Standing on the threshold of his life's calling, Hauge pondered the great spiritual need of Norway. Could God do in other parts what He had done in his own community? He thought so.

But before he could travel and witness he would have to get his book printed. It was a personal testimony of his conversion entitled *The Foolishness of the World*. One of the reasons he had written this book was to help counteract the false rumors that had circulated about him.

The journey to Oslo, a distance of about 60 miles, was unusual in that during that time he was almost overwhelmed with thoughts of doubt and despair. Conflicting voices raged within, "It is none of your business to write, speak about God, and teach others." But another voice countered by saying "You will lose your own soul unless you obey the voice of God." Several times on this journey he had to kneel and pray for strength and guidance.

Upon arriving in Oslo he soon found a printer who would publish his book, together with another booklet he had translated from the German, *Evangelical Rules of Life.*

In this inauspicious way a great literary career was launched. Without the benefit of dictionary or commentaries Hauge produced and printed more than a quarter of a million books, pamphlets, and tracts in his lifetime. At one time it required five printing presses working full time to take care of the demand. Colporteurs were kept busy carrying these books over mountains and through the valleys to people everywhere. It is no secret that people in the midst of a spiritual renewal are the most avid readers of all.

Having found a publisher for his books, he was now ready to begin his itinerant work as an evangelist. It would be rugged and demanding, but at age 25, he was strong and in the prime of his life.

The roads in those days were few and poor, and sometimes there were no roads at all. Occasionally Hauge had the luxury of riding horseback, but most of the time he was on foot. In order to make the best possible use of his time he would knit as he walked. Often it would be a pair of socks for himself or someone else. . .mostly for others.

Upon reaching a farmstead he would offer to help with the field work, splitting wood, or some other chore. In the evening a service would be held. If it was Sunday perhaps he would hold an afternoon service, but he was always careful not to interfere with any of the regular church services. He always encouraged the people to be loyal to the state church. They were encouraged to be regular in attendance, participate in the communion service and not to neglect the baptizing of their children. He was a good example of what he taught; when he was in a given community he could be found among the parishioners in the worship service.

The common people received him gladly. Not only did they attend his services in the homes, but they followed him as he walked from place to place, much as the people did in the days of Jesus.

For eight years he was able to carry on with his evangelistic labors. Walking 20 or more miles a day he would hold as many as four services. These gatherings were times of refreshing. The Word was preached, sinners were converted, testimonies were shared and free prayer was offered. It was a new experience for the people to discover that religious life could be so fulfilling and satisfying.

This awakening was of a quiet order. The Moravians, of whom there were quite a number, were much more demonstrative in their faith. No so the Lutherans, yet they were equally well grounded in their relationship with God.

Towards the close of his evangelistic career he made a journey north as far as Tromso, north of the Arctic Circle. Daylight hours were few and the nights were long. He traveled miles and miles over untrodden snow fields, sleeping in the snow at night.

Not only were the elements against him, but so were the people. The opposition had been building until it was difficult for him or his followers, in their travels, to obtain either food or lodging. On this particular journey to Tromso it was the Laplanders who opened their doors and hearts to him.

Though Hauge had been accused of idleness, it is doubtful whether anyone in Norway had accomplished as much as he had. Besides sparking a religious revival that reached out into all parts of Norway, he had also been instrumental in setting up a paper mill, fanning mill, bone grinding mill, and a tannery.

During the Napoleonic wars the English Fleet had blockaded the coast of Norway. It was a very difficult time for the people. At this time Hauge was released from prison so that he could supervise the setting up of salt plants in various parts of the country. During the dreadful famine of 1812 he spent his time assisting the poor. He had hired a girl to provide the needy with food staples such as flour, herring, and potatoes.

In spite of the good that had been accomplished, both in a temporal and spiritual way, Hauge found himself in more and more trouble. He had not only incurred the wrath of the clergy, but now the governing and business classes were angry with him too. Their greed and insensitivity to the needs of others had been exposed by his benevolence. Though he was no stranger to jails and sheriffs the gathering clouds of a more permanent incarceration loomed on the horizon. Under the dateline of June 30, 1804, the government issued an order to all bishops and sheriffs to provide as much information as possible about "this dangerous movement" and requested help as to how it could be curbed, and if possible, stopped. The charges against him were the usual ones such as being "a fanatic, a deceiver, a rogue. . .traitor, whose chief aim is to come into possession of the property of his adherents."[4]

On October 24, 1804, Hauge was arrested, imprisoned and placed in shackles in the Haugesund jail. "But," said Hauge, "that night I slept better than I had done for a long time, knowing that I had a good conscience and my aim had been to do that which was good only."

November 24 he was transferred to Oslo. His treatment here was unusually harsh. After only one year his health was broken, but his greatest distress was the thought that perhaps God had forsaken him.

About a year had elapsed when an incident took place which

was to have far reaching consequences. It was Christmas Eve. At the prison gate were two of his friends waiting to see him, Ole Roersveen and Sampson Trae. Roersveen was the colporteur whose back was bent from carrying Hauge's books. One of them inquired from the chief of police if they could see the prisoner. The answer was a brisk refusal. "Only a couple of words," pleaded the little man. Again, the answer was an emphatic "No!" Was there nothing they could do, they pondered among themselves? Then a thought occurred. Christmas was a time of joy and singing. They would sing a song. Perhaps he would hear them.

When their singing subsided they looked up at the prison window. Suddenly a light appeared. He *had* heard them. Then for a moment it disappeared, only to reappear again in a few minutes. Now the wick had been trimmed. Shining more brightly, the lesson was obvious. The church needed to be cleansed so it could shine more brightly. What a message! His followers never forgot.

Hauge's prison term had come to an end after 10 years. He was now a free man. Friends helped him purchase a farm outside Oslo. It became a center of Christian activity. But Hauge was no longer the strong, robust man of earlier years. Travel was now out of the question, but he ministered in his own home as strength would allow.

He had never married as a young man, but now at the age of 44 he was united in marriage to Andrea Nyhus. Their life together was short-lived. His wife, after only a year, died giving birth to their son. Later he married Ingeborg Oldsdatter, who would be his companion and comforter in the remaining years of his life. He was only 53 when he was called home. His last words were, "Follow Jesus," and "Oh thou eternal and merciful God."

The respect and recognition that had been denied him in earlier days came to him in his declining years. He was looked upon as a martyr. People of all classes came to see him at his farm. They were greatly touched by contact with this godly man.

His place in Norway's history can be better understood when we read Norway's official publication for the Paris Exposition in 1900. Under an article entitled "Literature," page 495, we read:

"The political emancipation (of 1814) was accompanied by a regeneration of the religious life among the people in a revival that was led by the 'Peasant Apostle,' Hans Nielsen Hauge."

There is also the crowning moment of vindication that came to him posthumously when the religious leaders of Norway, in the dark days of World War II, issued a proclamation to the people admonishing them to adhere to the "Old Haugeen line" and the fundamental Bible position of the Reformation.

[1]P. Ljostveit, *Inner Mission Church History*, p. 378.
[2]Willhelm Petterson, *The Light in the Prison Window*, p. 24.
[3]Petterson, p. 53.
[4]Ljostveit, p. 153.

18

Samuel Morris
(1872-1893)

Methodist

On the campus of Taylor University in Upland, Indiana, lingers the memory of a man who, for a few brief months, lived and walked among the students on the old campus at Fort Wayne. Like a meteor from heaven he came and then was gone, but not before he had left a foretaste of what heaven is like.

Samuel Morris (his African name was Kaboo) was born on the Ivory Coast of Africa in 1872. As a child he came to know first hand the tortures of savage warfare. His father, a petty chieftain, was the vanquished leader in three successive wars and each time, as was the custom in tribal warfare, the oldest son was taken as a pawn until the proper war reparations could be made. He was only a child the first time, and was shortly released when the tribute was paid. The second time he was held captive for several years and suffered immeasurably at the hands of the bestial victors. The victorious tribesmen always made sure that their vanquished enemy was kept informed as to how their captive was being treated. The cruelty would become progressively worse from day to day. The purpose, of course, was to expedite the bringing forth of the tribute that would set the captive free.

Kaboo was 15 when he was carried away captive for the third time. The tribe was unable to pay the exorbitant ransom levied upon them, and the enemy tribe proceeded to apply the necessary pressure which would somehow produce the ransom. First there was the ritual of daily beatings. Each time they became more severe. When a captive was no longer able to stand, he would be laid on a cross tree and beaten into unconsciousness. The form of torture, which was the final one, was to bury the victim with only his head above the ground. His mouth was kept open with a stick and smeared with something sweet. The driver ants would be attracted to the helpless victim and consume his flesh. Then the skeleton would be put on display for all to see. They had progressed so far as to place young Kaboo on the cross tree when a bright light appeared, enveloping his body, and a voice commanded him to flee. He obeyed the voice and ran. That night he found shelter in a hollow tree. The following day he continued on his journey, led by a mysterious light that shone in the darkened forest. Though it was a land of cannibals and wild beasts and crawling with poisonous snakes, he was never harmed. After weeks of walking he came to a plantation just outside of Monrovia, Liberia, where he found employment.

That first Sunday morning found him in a Christian service for the first time in his life. The missionary was speaking through an interpreter and telling them about Paul, his conversion, and the light that shone about him. The young lad became excited. "I have seen that light," he exclaimed. "It was the same light that brought me here."

Though he was now a Christian, he was awakened to a greater need in his life. His dark past bothered him. His desire for revenge haunted him. To assuage the inner burden of his heart, he spent much time in prayer.

One night he had a remarkable experience. His room was filled with light. Instantly his burden was lifted, and he was filled with such ecstasy that his shouts awakened everyone in the barracks.

This divine visitation resulted in a yet deeper commitment to his Lord, and he was led to understand that what had happened to him was the work of the Holy Spirit. How he read with renewed interest such portions of Scripture as John 14, which spoke of an indwelling Christ.

The young African joined the Methodist church in Monrovia, and it was there that he acquired the name of Samuel Morris. It has been a common practice on the mission fields of the world that when the heathen are converted to Christianity they take for themselves a new name, often a Bible name. In Kaboo's case, it was Miss Knool who persuaded him to adopt the name of Samuel Morris. She herself was indebted to an American banker by that name who had so kindly assisted her financially in her student years. It was her way of expressing her gratitude for his kindness and generosity.

Morris' interest in spiritual things continued to grow. He was especially taken up with the subject of the Holy Spirit. His most recent encounter had wedded him to a diligent research of the subject. When he wasn't working or reading he was badgering the Christian workers to tell him more about this third person of the Trinity.

Finally, a friend, who was no longer able to answer his many questions, suggested that if he wanted more answers he would have to go and talk to a certain Stephen Merritt in New York. This was, of course, an impossibility. The worker knew it. But he underestimated the lad's determination and the providence of God. His instant reply was, "I will go to New York to see him," and within a short time he was bound for the seacoast and a sailing vessel anchored in the harbor. Approaching the captain of the ship he said, "My father in heaven told me you would take me to New York. I want to see Stephen Merritt who lives there." "You are crazy," replied the captain.

Morris was not to be denied. Day after day he approached the captain, and each time he was refused. Finally he came to him again: "My father tells me you will take me now." Some of the crew had deserted and the captain needed replacements, so Morris was hired. As he came aboard ship he saw a crewman lying on the deck, injured and unable to get up. As Morris knelt down and asked God to heal him, he was instantly restored.

The six month sea voyage did not begin on a pleasant note for the newly recruited seaman. The captain had assumed that he had taken aboard an experienced hand, and when he learned that Morris knew nothing about the duties aboard a sailing vessel he was furious. He was about to send him ashore when one of the regular seamen, the one who had just been prayed for, cried out, "Please keep him, he has done so much for me." Reluctantly, the captain, after administering a few blows to the head, allowed him to remain.

It would be difficult to find a more motley assortment of men than comprised this crew. They were ungodly drunkards and potential killers. One of these, in a drunken frenzy with cutlass in hand, was inching forward on deck toward some of his shipmates. As Morris stepped between them with the cry, "Don't kill, don't kill!" the half-crazed giant, who had especially hated Morris, was stopped in his tracks. He dropped his weapon and returned to his quarters. Hearing the commotion on deck, the captain came to quell the storm, only to find that Morris had it well in hand.

After order was restored, Morris went below deck, where he knelt by his bunk and began to pray for all aboard. The captain, under the spell of the mighty calm that had taken over on topside, followed Morris below deck. When the young lad knelt to pray, so did the captain. He thereupon began to pray, (probably for the first time) and thanked God for sending the young man among them. The captain was, from that day on, an entirely changed man. The drunken brawls gave way to prayer services among the men. Rum, the curse aboard every sailing vessel, was no longer dispensed, and order and harmony followed. The drunken sailor who was responsible for all the commotion was later stricken with what appeared to be a fatal illness. Again Morris rose to the occasion and called upon his God, who again answered by restoring the penitent sailor to health.

The six month journey, which had begun under such adverse circumstances for Morris, culminated in a climate of such love and triumph that, when he was leaving the ship, many of the crewmen wept. The young man had opened their eyes to a way of life such as they had never known before. Years later the sea captain, in conversing with Stephen Merritt, wept when he heard of Morris' passing some years before. He informed the mission worker that most of the sailors were still with him, and that the saintly influence of Morris had brought a permanent reformation among them.

Morris was again on his own, this time in the largest city of the land. He was without a contact or an address. How could he possibly find Stephen Merritt?

On stepping ashore he approached the first person he saw. "Where can I find Stephen Merritt?" The stranger, a tramp, knew where the mission was. He had also met Merritt. He would take him there for a dollar. Morris agreed and they were on their way.

On arriving at the mission Morris wasted no time. "I am Samuel Morris," he said. "I have come from Africa to talk to you about the Holy Spirit." "I want my dollar," interrupted the bum. Morris replied, "Stephen Merritt pays my bills." His new host obliged with a smile, and the guide was on his way.

It turned out to be a memorable evening. Morris was left for the time being at the mission where the evening service was already in progress. When Merritt returned he saw Morris standing up front with 17 young men on their knees, tears streaming down their faces, seeking God.

It was past midnight when Merritt arrived at home with his new found friend. The new surroundings and private room bewildered him. He had never seen such beautiful accommodations, and in fact had to be helped by his host to prepare for the night.

The following day Merritt was to conduct a funeral. He took Morris with him. On the way the carriage picked up two more ministers who were to participate in the funeral. Merritt, feeling somewhat apologetic for having brought the poorly clad black boy with him, tried to put every one at ease with small talk, and from time to time pointed out to Morris various landmarks of importance in the big metropolis.

Morris was not impressed. He had not come from Africa to see the sights of New York City. A momentary pause gave him his opportunity. Addressing Merritt he said, "Have you ever prayed in a coach?" "No," Merritt replied. "We will pray," said the lad, and Merritt stopped the horses and knelt. Morris began to talk to the Lord. He told his Father that he had come to see Merritt so that he might learn more about the Holy Ghost, but that he had met with disappointment. Instead, he complained, he had been shown the city with its large buildings, churches, harbor and banks, but up to now he had not heard anything about the Holy Spirit. Now, the lad pleaded, "fill him with Thyself so that he will not think, talk, write, or preach about anything else."

The experience was an unforgettable one for Merritt. He had been ushered beyond embarrassment to where the reality of God is to be found. That funeral sermon came fresh from the fountain head with unerring accuracy, piercing many as they knelt by the casket and repented of their sins and waywardness.

The following Sunday Morris was asked to speak on the Holy Spirit in Sunday School. Having such a stranger in their midst brought smiles and myrth to the assembled students. But their levity was short lived. The African boy had spoken only a few minutes when the children began to weep.

Merritt recommended that Morris be sent to Taylor University to obtain an education. This was highly unorthodox. What little training he had obtained in Monrovia was very elementary. But a number of young ladies came to the rescue and offered to tutor him in preparation for the college level courses.

From the very beginning he stirred the hearts of the faculty and students. His humility, his transparency and his simple faith in God was without equal. He gave them a glimpse of what heaven must be like. He might have needed tutors to help him in his secular studies, but in his walk with God he was everyone's teacher.

His first Sunday in Fort Wayne found him in a black church. Though arriving late he proceeded to introduce himself to the pastor and people as Samuel Morris from Africa, and stated that he had a message for them. Though he had interrupted the morning service so unceremoniously, the pastor allowed him to continue. He had only spoken a few minutes when the same mysterious power enveloped the congregation, and they were on their knees weeping over their sins, or rejoicing over what God was doing.

Morris became ill in the winter of that year. Though only 21, his frail constitution was no match for the extreme climate, and slowly his body wasted away. He prayed to be healed but was not. One day his Father revealed to him, "that soon he would be in the city where the inhabitants shall not say, 'I am sick.'" Now he was at peace.

Someone else would go to bring the Gospel to his people. When he passed away two young men offered their services to Morris' homeland, and others followed.

The body of Samuel Morris lies buried in Lindenwood Cemetery in Fort Wayne, Indiana. Thousands have journeyed there just to see the final resting place of this young lad, and to catch, if possible, something of that spirit that moved so mightily in this "Angel in Black."

19

George Fox (1624-1690)

Quaker

The stinking prison cell was no Hilton suite, but neither was the occupant there by choice. He was there because of the discomfort he had brought to others. Was he a criminal? On the contrary, he belonged to that group of godly men who helped to shape the destiny of their land. His presence among the people, however, was often the signal for an uproar, and soon the sheriff or magistrate was there to cart him off to jail.

George Fox blossomed in a most unlikely setting. The embers of the Reformation had all but died out. The great Puritan Movement that had risen up to maintain the simplicity of the Gospel had also its day. It had become negative, stern, and uncompromising. It was overly occupied with denunciations and external habits of behavior and dress.

It was, therefore, a dark day into which George Fox had been ushered. The church was impotent and blase. Formalism had, by and large, taken over the church, and infidelity the world. Then upon the horizon appeared a man. . .a prophet of God to the nations.

George Fox was born in Leicestershire, England, in 1624. His parents were devout Christians and members of the Church of England. When George was 11 years of age he committed his life to Christ, and from that day continued steadfast, with the light he had, in his pursuit of God. He resolved that he would live a pure and righteous life, would be faithful in all things, and would be a man who kept his word. He also would practice moderation in his eating and drinking habits. These two latter resolves were in direct opposition to the spirit of the day.

Fox had little formal education. He was trained in the shoemaking profession, but when he was 19 his restless soul took leave of his surroundings, and he began to wander from place to place, just so he could be alone with God.

Up to this time, his Christian experience had not been a satisfactory one. The void in his heart belied the promised peace spoken of in the Bible. What was even worse was that no one seemed able to help him. No one had what he was looking for. There were times when his hopes and expectations would rise when he heard of some man with a spiritual reputation, but upon meeting him and conversing with him, he was disappointed and went on his way.

For instance, he visited a pastor who was highly recommended as being a spiritual man. They stood conversing in the flower garden, and all went well until Fox inadvertently. stepped on one of the flower plants. This drew the ire of the clergyman, and a disillusioned George Fox walked sadly away.

Help from his fellow man was never forthcoming and in later years he understood why. He had been prevented from leaning on man that he might learn to lean wholly on God. From that time on he ceased to accept any help from either the Church of England or the free churches (dissenters), and instead resolved to resign himself to God and take the Scriptures as his guide.

Shortly thereafter the truth became evident to him. He saw that the Lord had been waiting for him all the time. It was then that he heard a voice saying, "There is one, even Christ Jesus, who can speak to thy condition." It was pointed out to him that the reason he had not found any help from man was in order that the credit for his deliverance should be given to God, and that Jesus Christ should henceforth have the preeminence in his life.

Strangely enough, this encounter with God, beautiful at first, led him into a valley of great darkness and temptation. He began to question whether or not, in his exuberance, he might have sinned against God. He was perplexed and sad. Again he had no recourse but to go to God.

One day as he was out walking by himself, the darkness lifted and sunlight flooded his soul. For the time being it seemed as if there were only two personalities in the universe—he and God. It was that close, personal encounter that changes a man for all time. He had gazed into eternity, looked into the universe of God, and felt a part of it. But, best of all, he had his encounter with the risen Lord. In that hour he was shown Christ's part and man's part in the plan of redemption. He was given to undertstand that the fires of persecution he had been passing through were intended for his good, to make him strong. It was a memorable day, never to be forgotten. One writer gives us the closing scene: "His eyes were as yet closed as he stood in the open field under the calm sky, his soul naked and alone before his Creator."[1]

There were two illusions that ensnared the people of that time. The first was that all church members were believers and were on their way to heaven. The other, that if the pastor had been educated at Oxford or Cambridge he was qualified to be a minister of Jesus Christ. As he studied the Scriptures he began to see the folly of such teaching.

Walking alone in the country Fox constantly pondered the Scriptures. God would give him "openings," he said, meaning that the Spirit of God would throw light on some previously hidden truth in Scriptures, and it would become alive and real to him.

One such revelation to his soul was that the so-called church building was not the church. Instead, the church consisted of people. . .believers. *They* were the dwelling place of God. *They* were his temple. What men called churches, he called "steeple-houses."

As God continued to lead him and instruct him, he was led to see that two laws governed and controlled men, the law of the flesh and the law of the Spirit. The natural man was governed by the law of the flesh, but the believer who was indwelt by the Spirit of God had the ability to live above the flesh and its works, if so desired.

Fox was in his early 20's when he emerged from his period of desolation. And now with the new found joy, liberty and freedom, he began to share his experiences with others. He had much to give. Since he now saw clearly God's part and man's part in salvation, he was able to share it freely with the hungry souls about him. But he didn't stop there. He went on to teach that God wanted men to be holy and pure in heart. They were to love each other as well as God. He spoke of perfection and the inner light. They might call him the unlearned shoe cobbler, but the clergy were hard pressed to match him in argument.

The multitudes were now beginning to give him a listening ear, as did the clergy. What they heard upset them. They had been taught that sin and imperfection were part of the Christian life. They had come to the service assuming, as they always had, that they were Christians, only to find out from this man that they did not qualify for heaven after all.

This revelation left them in shock. Terrible conviction came as a result. "The power of the Lord," said Fox, "was dreadful among them in the steeple-houses, so that the people trembled and shook; some of them feared that it would fall down on their heads."

Fox's reputation now went before him. "And now," he said, "I went into the country and had mighty great meetings. The everlasting Gospel and Word of Life flourished and thousands were turned to the Lord Jesus Christ and to His teaching."

In the early days of his ministry Fox passed through a remarkable experience which had much to do with his future success as a preacher. A certain man by the name of Brown had prophesied on his deathbed great things concerning Fox.

When the man passed away the prophetic mantle seemed to have fallen on Fox. He became a changed man. He was given a spirit of discernment in which he saw people speak about God and Christ, but it was in reality the serpent speaking through them. This was, at first, difficult for him to believe, yet he saw the character of some as being "like that of a fox, like a wolf, a serpent, a lion or a wasp, etc."

Having such insight into the character of the people would undoubtedly influence his preaching and offend many. Consequently he was often before magistrates and spent much time in jail.

Not only did he lack formal training for the ministry, he also had no particular qualities of leadership, except his example. He began without a single follower. It was not uncommon for him to stand up at the close of a service and challenge the minister or the people who had been listening. Pandemonium often followed, and then the jailhouse for Fox. But he got their attention. From no followers at all, he slowly gathered a people so totally changed and committed that the authorities were hard pressed to know what to do with them. Their righteous lives condemned those about them. Many of them, also, went to prison. No religious renewal, as far as we know, had such a large percentage of its constituency behind prison bars. It is estimated that in 1662 there were 4,500 Quakers in prison in England and Wales.

The persecutions in America were even more severe. The

one great object of this 17th century reformer was to turn the eyes of the people away from outward forms and ceremonies, and to direct their attention to the real need which was holiness. He seems to have patterned his ministry after Christ in that respect. He, too, was a reformer with not much regard to the outward forms and ceremonies of his day.

As a monument to this servant of God and his work, there are multitudes of people around the world today who call themselves Quakers or Friends. Many others have been influenced by his teachings, though they are in other folds.

The world owes a debt of gratitude to Fox and his followers. They spoke out against slavery 200 years before anyone else. They have been consistently opposed to carrying arms. God honored this faith. It is a matter of record that the Quakers never lost a man, woman, or child in the Indian uprisings in our country. They were also the early champions of women's rights. Consequently, many of the women among them became evangelists, ministers, and teachers. They have also been instrumental in helping to secure the abolition of capitol punishment for minor offenses. It is no doubt that their stand for freedom of Christian expression has had much to do with the freedom of religion we enjoy today.

[1]Major Douglas, *George Fox, The Red-Hot Quaker*, p. 14.

20

Ann Preston
(Holy Ann)
(1810-1906)

Methodist

Scribbled in chalk marks on the door were these words: "Holy Ann lives here. Go in and have a word of prayer." The intended victim went to God for herself and the guilty pranksters and her prayer was, "Oh, Father, they are calling me Holy Ann. Make me holy so the children will not be telling lies."

Holy Ann, whose real name was Ann Preston, was born about 1810 in the small village of Ballamacally in the county of Armagh in Ireland. She was in every sense a child of poverty. Her home was an Irish shanty. Her formal schooling consisted of about one week of academic training. On her final day of school her distraught teacher tapped her on the head and said, "Poor Ann, she can never learn anything." Thereupon she was dismissed and sent home in disgrace.

She was equally poor in the things of the Spirit. Neither her father nor mother made any claim to piety, and consequently their five children, Ann included, were as innocent as babes in spiritual matters.

The young Irish girl was no saint by nature, but the divine apparatus for retrieving lost sinners came into operation in her home. First of all there was her own conscience that would trouble her at times about her childhood wrongdoing. Then there was a godly aunt who had come to live in the home for a season. Preston's sister, Mary, traced the beginning of her sister's spiritual life to this period.

Preston had left home early in life to work for others, first as a babysitter and later tending and herding cattle. But her surroundings were not conducive to any kind of spiritual development. There was no opportunity, that is, until she was offered employment with a Christian lady named Mrs. McKay.

McKay was also Irish—and a Methodist. Family prayer, which was observed every day, was something new for Preston. Though alert and anxious to win all her help to God, McKay was also judicious and patient, waiting for the opportune time. Only after some time had elapsed did she venture to invite Preston to a Methodist class meeting. What she saw was all new to her. But the weeping of some, and others praising God, confounded and offended her. She questioned their sincerity, although she said nothing.

Later that day McKay invited Preston into the parlor for conversation. McKay asked her what she thought of the meeting. Preston was reluctant to say anything. She finally admitted that she felt out of place since she had nothing to say. Upon being asked if she would like to go again she replied firmly, "I don't think so."

McKay, however, did not give up. The following Sunday service was scheduled to be held in the neighbor's home. She persuaded Preston to go with her. Those were the days when the Methodists were a poor and despised sect. They had no church buildings, so they met in homes instead. Preston remembered little of the service except the text the minister had used. "Thou, when thou prayest, enter into thy closet, and when thou hast shut the door, pray to thy father who seeth in secret and thy Father who seeth in secret shall reward thee openly" (Matthew 6:6).

After the evening chores were completed, Preston made her way to the attic on the third floor of the house. It was a large room with only one piece of furniture, a large wooden chair. Here she knelt for the first time in her life and began to cry unto God. She had no conception of what was wrong, what she wanted, or what was needed. All she knew was that she had an intolerable burden, too heavy for her to bear.

Her heart-rending cries could be heard three floors down. Upon hearing the commotion upstairs, McKay went up to see if she could be of help. When she asked Preston what was the matter she replied, "I don't know Ma'am." But in the next breath she said, "Oh, yes I do. I see all the sins that ever I did, from the time I was five years old, all written on the chair in front of me, every one." As she looked down she cried out, "Oh, Ma'am, worse than all, I see hell open, ready to swallow me." Then, without ever having heard or read the particular Scripture, she began to beat her breast and cry out, "God be merciful to me, a sinner." McKay did not want her husband to hear the tumult that was going on, so she suggested that Preston go to her own room and pray quietly and she would likewise go to her room and pray for her. To this she replied, "I don't care, Ma'am, if all the world hears me; I must cry for mercy."

She returned to her room and continued to pray, but found no relief. It was midnight when she abruptly rose, and as she did she asked the question, "No mercy for me, Lord?" In that moment her burden lifted and she saw and understood the scheme of redemption. She had not been forgotten. She had been provided for. She said, "I felt something burning in my heart." Then she added, "I just longed for the morning that I could go home and tell my father and mother what the Lord had done for me."

This was followed by a most remarkable phenomenon. She picked up a New Testament and, as she did, she prayed, "Oh, Lord, you that have taken away this awful burden, intolerable to bear, couldn't you enable me to read one of these little things?" As she did this she put her finger on a verse which read, "Whosoever drinketh of this water shall thirst again, but whosoever drinketh of the water that I shall give shall never thirst" (John 4:13, 14). For the first time in her life she was able to read. She did not understand the whole verse, but it was the beginning of a learning experience which enabled her to read the Word of God.

Any other literature or newspaper was unintelligible. Once, in attempting to decipher some words in the newspaper, she found a word that seemed to read "lord," but she quickly added, "I don't think it is my 'Lord' as my heart doesn't burn while I see it." Checking the newspaper more carefully it was found that the article referred to a report on the South African war in which reference was made to the achievements of a "Lord" Roberts.

It was the afternoon of the following day before she had opportunity to go home and tell her parents what had happened. As many a beginner in the Christian life knows, such an experience is a time of real testing. On the way there the enemy whispered, "You don't feel the burning in your heart now. You had better not say anything about it until you are sure."

Her mind, however, was fixed, and her determination prevailed. The news was received with silence. Finally her mother responded, "Oh, you are like your old grandfather. You are going out of your head." Like many new converts she had set out to convert the world only to find there was little or no interest in the message.

Crestfallen, but not defeated, she took heart when a letter from her sister had the following lines in it: "I am sure you have good news to tell me, Ann. I know by the answer I have gotten in prayer." What was amazing to Ann was that the letter had been written two days before she had begun to cry to God for salvation.

After leaving the McKay home Preston found employment with the family of a Dr. Reid. Her salary was two dollars per month. Though she had been a Christian for a number of years, she had made little progress beyond the elementary stage of initial salvation. She was still, as Paul said of the Corinthians, a babe in Christ. Not being grounded in the Word of God, she was often at the mercy of her feelings. As she listened to others and their testimonies she would be vicariously carried upward on the breezes of ecstasy, but more often she would find herself in the trough of despair.

Circumstances in the Reid home seemed to have tried her. There were times when she contemplated suicide. On one such occasion she actually took steps to destroy herself. Reid had procurred a very vicious cow and hardly anyone dared come near her. It was Preston's job to milk this cow, but in order to do so someone always went along to hold her. On this particular occasion Preston slipped out earlier than usual, and walked the mile to where the cow was kept. She fully expected the brute would turn on her, and do away with her, when she attempted to milk her. Instead, however, she stood perfectly still through the entire milking session. This convinced her that the Lord was indeed watching over her, and from that day her better judgment prevailed. She would no longer presume upon His protection, but always took someone with her to hold the cow at milking time.

After five years of working in the Reid household, a new adventure beckoned her. Reid and his family were moving to Canada, and they invited her to go with them. Her parents and loved ones tried to persuade her not to go, but she was determined. She felt an obligation to the Reid household. Her sister, seeing that she would not be deterred, gave her a verse of Scripture as they parted: "Hold thou fast which thou hast, that no man take thy crown." The passage did not mean much to Preston at the time, but in years to come she would learn to cherish and appreciate it.

Preston was busy during the seven weeks at sea. She had the care of three households, and they were all sick. Responding to an inquiry as to whether she had not also been ill she replied, "Sure, I had no time to get seasick."

The sailing vessel finally entered New York harbor and the Hudson River. From Albany, the Reid household went overland to Toronto. After a few months the doctor moved his family to Thornhill where he took up his practice.

Five years had elapsed when Reid suddenly died. It was an unexpected shock to the whole household. This placed a great burden on Preston who now had the sole charge of this large household. It was a trying time for her. She did not have the spiritual resources to cope with the daily tasks and the problems that went with them. Reid, the good Methodist that he was and leader of the Bible class in church, was also deficient in certain Christian virtues. Perhaps he did not see his inconsistencies, but Preston did. Her progress toward spiritual maturity, however, was equally minimal.

Her contribution to the bedlam in the Reid household was a volatile Irish temper and on one occasion, after the battle was over, it took two weeks before the frost thawed and normal relations were restored. In later years she described her life during that period as "truly awful, sinning and repenting, sinning and repenting."

Had her life ended here there would have been little to record. But a great change came over her and the explosive temper which was her greatest liability was, in a moment, conquered and sublimated. The lass who had been unable to read now became a wellspring of Scripture, applying the texts to the occasions at hand. In addition she began to experience remarkable answers to prayer. Consistently the answers would come as she presented her requests before the throne of God.

One day a young man came to their home. Before retiring for the evening he led the family in worship, reading the 34th Psalm. "The face of the Lord is against them that do evil, to cut off the remembrance of them from the earth." Preston asked the young man to mark the passage for her. She then went to her room where she knelt and asked God for further help and understanding. As she opened her Bible to read the particular passage, the enemy challenged her by reminding her that she couldn't read. To which she replied, "Well, the Lord will give it to me." And so He did. From that day she was able to read her Bible accurately.

Though she could now read there were many things she did not understand. All night she remained on her knees asking God questions and pondering the answers that He gave her. But by morning's light she had not yet been able to find rest for her soul. She was, however, a determined lass. "I'll die, but I'll have it," she said as she arose from her knees to go downstairs.

The young man was already up, and when she entered the room he asked her why she had been crying all night. She replied, "I want to be sanctified throughout, body, soul, and spirit." His reply was, "Well, Ann, how were you justified?" She replied, "Why, just believing what God said." "Well," he said, "complete victory comes in the same way."

She went back to prayer and pleaded the promise, "Ask and it shall be given you, seek and ye shall find, knock and it shall be opened unto you." She then reminded the Lord that she had been knocking all night and thus far no answer had been forthcoming. But in that moment the answer came. Her eyes were opened, and she was instantly changed.

It was as though she had been transported to heaven. Her vocal exuberance soon awakened the household. She was so excited that for eight days she was unable to eat. It was a remarkable and enduring experience.

For over seven years she lived in this euphoric frame of mind.

She would awaken in the morning and find herself in such a happy state of mind that she would sit up in bed and clap her hands as she began her conscious communion with the Lord.

Some days had passed when she awakened one morning to find her usual joy missing. The temptation came, "You have lost your blessing." However, she fell back to sleep. She dreamed she was conversing with another woman who had had the same experience. Now she saw herself counseling the other woman to walk by faith. Upon awakening she "turned the sermon on herself" and peace of mind was restored.

The change that came over Preston did not go unnoticed. From a life of struggle and defeat .she stepped out into the sunshine of power and blessing. Soon others were coming to her for counsel and advice, but most of all they sought her prayers. She prayed about everything. . .and God heard and answered. There were times, however, when prayers seemed to go unanswered, but she was to learn that this, too, was a part of her schooling.

One such incident involved an ankle injury she sustained as a result of jumping over a fence and twisting her ankle. Infection set in and she was incapacitated for over a year. The God who can heal ankles in an instant did not do so in her case. Instead He used the seeming misfortune to instruct Preston and draw her closer to Himself.

Weakened by the ordeal, the doctor prescribed fresh eggs and milk to her diet. But it was in the dead of winter and the hens were not laying. There was not one egg to be found in the entire village.

This became an object of prayer for Preston. The answer came when a hen strutted into the house, deposited an egg, and went out without making a sound. This continued for three weeks. At the end of that time there was no further need for eggs, and the special provision ceased.

Her life was a life of constant communion with God. Prayer was her special forte. Children, not to mention adults, would come to her because something had been lost. Preston would pray and the Lord would tell her where the object was.

One summer the well went dry. Preston prayed, and the next morning there was an abundant supply of sparkling water. Her home was about one-fourth of a mile back from the road. Come winter with its heavy snows there was no way she could get out. But she would ask her heavenly Father, and usually someone would come and shovel the path. One time, however, no one came. But she had asked and was confident the answer would be forthcoming. Later in the day, hearing the laughter and shouting of the children outside, she looked through her window and there she saw a beautiful sight. Five prancing horses were running back and forth in a straight line between the house and the road, leaving a cleared path.

Preston was an ardent witness for her Lord, and when testimony time came she would share and exhort. Once she went to a Catholic cathedral with her friend. They were ushered into one of the front pews. The service was much different from the Methodist service she was accustomed to. Preston, however, kept her poise as she listened to the bishop contrast Roman Catholicism with the Protestant churches. The bishop took each denomination, one by one, and gave the historical background together with its weaknesses as compared to the Catholic church. Preston was neither impressed nor disturbed until he came to the Methodist church. Now she was all ears. She detected inaccuracies in his discourse, and immediately rose to refute and correct the good bishop.

The assembled congregation was shocked. Nothing like this had ever happened before. Her friend was mortified. Reaching out she tried to pull her down into her seat, but Preston wasn't through. Now she had two adversaries to contend with. Looking down at her friend she said, "Stop plucking me, I am not a goose."

Preston died January 25, 1906, at the age of 96. The Berkely St. Methodist Church was packed for her funeral. Ministers from six different denominations paid fitting tribute and acknowledged how her life had influenced them.

Conclusion

We have now seen how the power of God can change and transform character. The men and women who make up this narrative were mostly ordinary folk, but they matured to become giants in their time. Their achievements were not those of works, but of faith. It was not what *they* did, but what they believed *God* could do that made them such outstanding men and women in their day.

Coming to maturity, however, was not easy. Time and patience must have their day in court. Almost without exception the individual will attempt to *save* himself or later to make himself holy. The experience is a horrendous eye opener. The magnitude of the task overwhelms him. It can only lead to despair, but it is the kind of despair that leads to the door of hope—the promise of a new day.

It was the revelation of God's grace to their hearts that enabled them to understand the Scriptures more clearly. They had been trying man's way; now they were beginning to see

God's way. What had been so dark and complex before was now readily understood. Now the words of the saintly writer, Hannah Whithall Smith, took on a new meaning: "All that we claim then," she once said, "in this life of sanctification is, that by an act of faith we put ourselves into the hands of the Lord. . .and then by a continuous exercise of faith keep ourselves there. This is our part in the matter."

Having thus made that total commitment to God, and having believed Him for the fulfillment of the promise of His indwelling presence, they then became radiant ambassadors for Him. They had found the rest that faith brings and had come into harmony with God and His universe. The reality of this divine—human relationship could not be hid, and the bystander could only stand in awe and concur with those of bygone days when they said of the disciples, "They took knowledge of them that they had been with Jesus."

Bibliography

Beech, Harry, *Back to the Faith*, Montrose, The Pilot Press, 1928.

Bingham, Helen E., *An Irish Saint*, New York, Evangelical Publishers, Inc., 1927.

Bunyan, John, *Pilgrim's Progress*, Grand Rapids, Zondervan Publishing Co.

Chambers, Oswald, *Oswald Chambers, His Life and Work*, London, Simkin Marshall, Ltd., 1933.

Cobb, E. Howard, *Christ Healing*, London, Marshall Morgan and Scott Ltd., 1933.

Collier, Richard, *The General Next to God*, New York, Dutton Publishing Co., 1965.

Day, Richard Ellsworth, *Bush Aglow*, Grand Rapids, Baker Book House, 1936.

Day, Richard Ellsworth, *Man of Like Passions*, Grand Rapids, Zondervan Publishing Co.

Douglas, Major, *George Fox, The Red Hot Quaker*, Cincinnati, God's Bible School and Missionary Training Home.

Earl, A.B., *Bringing in the Sheaves*, 1868.

Edman, V. Raymond, *They Found the Secret*, Grand Rapids, Zondervan Publishing House, 1960.

Finney, Charles G., *Charles Finney*, New York, Fleming H. Revell, 1876.

Frodsham, Stanley Howard, *Smith Wigglesworth—Apostle of Faith*, Springfield, Gospel Publishing House, 1948.

Guyon, Madam, *Madam Guyon*, Chicago, Moody Press.

Harvey/Hey, *They Knew Their God*, Burslem, M.O.V.E. Press, 1974.

Havergal, Frances, *Kept for the Master's Use*, Anderson, Warner Press, 1879.

Hills, A.M., *Holiness and Power*, Cincinnati, Revivalist Office.

Kazee, Buel H., *Faith is the Victory*, Grand Rapids, William B. Eerdmans Pub. Co., 1951.

Lawrence, Brother, *The Practice of the Presence of God*, New York, Fleming H. Revell Co., 1895.

Lawson, J. Gilchrist, *Deeper Experiences of Famous Christians*, Anderson, Warner Press, 1911.

Ljostveit, P., *Intermission Church History*, Hauge Innermission Federation, 1948.

Mantle, J. Gregory, *Beyond Humiliation*, Chicago, Moody Press

McGaw, Frances A., *Praying Hyde*, Minneapolis, Bethany Fellowship, Inc. 1970.

Miller, Basil, *George Muller*, Minneapolis, Bethany Fellowship, Inc.

Pettersen, Willhelm, *The Light in the Prison Window*, Minneapolis, K.C. Holter Publishing Co., 1921.

Report—*Student Mission Power*, Pasadena, William Carey Library, 1891.

Smith, Hannah Whithall, *The Christian's Secret of a Happy Life*.

Torrey, R.A., *Why God Used D.L. Moody*, Monroeville,

Banner Publications, 1923.

Tozer, A.W., *Wingspread*, Harrisburg, Christian
Publications, Inc., 1943.

Tozer, A.W., *The Pursuit of God*, Harrisburg, Christian
Publications, 1948.

Trumbull, Charles Gallaudet, "The Life That Wins"
Philadelphia, The Sunday School Times Co., 1956.

Wimberly, C.F., *Henry Clay Morrison*, Chicago, Fleming
H. Revell Co., 1922.

Wolf, Edmund Jacob, *The Lutherans in America*, New
York, J.A. Hill & Co., 1890.